Pearson's Canal Compan

STOURPORT RIN

Published by Central Waterways Supplies of Rugby
Tel/fax: 01788 546692 email: sales @centralwaterways.co.uk
Copyright: Michael Pearson - All rights reserved.
Sixth edition 2003. ISBN 0 9545383 1 5
Printed in Italy by STIGE of Torino

C000134738

tillerman

THERE I am, back again, on my beloved BCN: still crazy after all these locks; still wondering why I can never quite shake off the canals. Instead of life being one long round of coffee-table book launches and literary prize-winning acceptance speeches, I'm trudging the towpath, going over old ground: trying to fathom where British Telecom have moved that kiosk; trying to discover what artificially fizzy beer they serve at the Nailclipper & Cuticle now; wondering which side of the canal British Waterways have moved the visitor moorings. But they have their good points, these inland waterways; none more so than the BCN. And finding myself back in Great Bridge and Netherton and Pelsall again, it came upon me - ruefully - that there are many more tedious ways of eking out a living, and that I must not protest too vocally, lest the gods take umbrage and steer me on a much more irksome course than this. Go, enjoy yourselves. Discover what I discovered a decade ago, that the canals of the Trent and Severn valleys - and the Black Country between - are as beautiful and stimulating as you'll find anywhere in the world.

Michael Pearson

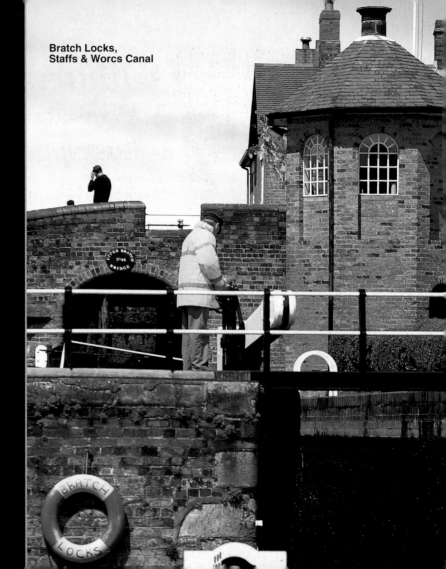

Bratch Locks,
Staffs & Worcs Canal

Stourport Ring

FOR all practical purposes, STOURPORT marks the head of navigation on the Severn, and it is here that the through traveller by water exchanges the fluctuating currents of the river for the stolid waters of the Staffordshire & Worcestershire Canal. Stourport itself suffers from a personality disorder: half convinced that it's a seaside town; half a rich heritage of canal wharves, vying with Shardlow on the Trent & Mersey Canal as the best preserved example of an early inland port.

But whether you have come here for a ninety-nine and a knees-up, or to pay more serious homage to Brindley's basins, Stourport rarely disappoints. To moor in the Upper Basin, listening to time being measured by the quarter beats of the clocktower's sonorous bell, is one of the inland waterways' most magical experiences. And whatever entrance the boater makes - locking up from the Severn under the benign gaze of the Tontine Hotel, or descending into the dripping depths of York Street lock from the canal - there will be few steerers able to resist exploration of the remaining basins, shunting back and forth like some busy tug; turning in wide arcs or honing their reversing skills. Remaining basins? Yes, there are four now, the original and largest - known as the Upper Basin - opened in 1771, and connects through two wide-beam 'barge' locks with the river. These impressive (at least in narrowboater's eyes) chambers were

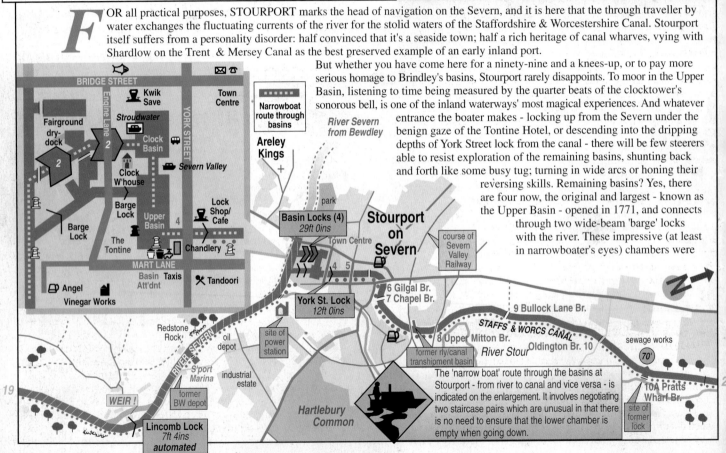

The 'narrow boat' route through the basins at Stourport - from river to canal and vice versa - is indicated on the enlargement. It involves negotiating two staircase pairs which are unusual in that there is no need to ensure that the lower chamber is empty when going down.

built sturdily enough to withstand the Severn's perennial propensity for flooding, and capacious enough for the indigenous Severn Trows. Between the barge locks lies the smallest surviving basin, thought to have been used as an assembly point and not as a wharf as such. A second link to the river, consisting of four narrow-beam locks in pairs of staircases, was opened in 1781. Here again the locks are separated by a small basin from which a drydock extends. Manoeuvring a lengthy boat between the staircase pairs can be tricky, and it doesn't help one's sang-froid that there is often a sizeable crowd of onlookers. At the top of the narrow locks, and contemporary with their construction, lies the Clock Basin, interconnected with the Upper Basin. On a peninsula between these upper, boat-filled expanses of water stands the glorious Clock Warehouse, headquarters these days of the Stourport Yacht Club whose comparatively huge vessels migrate up-river to winter in the security of the basins.

There are two lost basins which lay to the east of Mart Lane. Known expediently as the 'Furthermost Basins', they dated from the early 19th century. The lower, reached through a wide lock, had a brief existence, closing in 1866 when the town gas works took over the site. The other basin flourished in an Indian Summer of commercial activity between 1926 and 1949 when coal boats for the power station discharged in it; their dusty black cargoes of Cannock coalfield slack being unloaded by electric grab and carried in hoppers along an aerial ropeway to the power station's furnaces. A timber yard now covers the site of this basin, and only a tell-tale hump in an elusive alley leading from Mart Lane to the vinegar brewery hints at the existence of these forgotten docks.

The River

The Severn's official head of navigation is just upstream of Stourport Bridge where the Gladder Brook enters from the west bank, though occasional convoys of shallow-draughted diehards do journey upstream to Bewdley as part of a long term campaign to restore navigation to the Upper Severn all the way up to Shrewsbury; a relatively easy proposition were it not for the distrust of riparian landowners. One waterway project which did not materialise was for a canal from Stourport to Leominster. A token sod was dug opposite the basins in 1797, but the ludicrously ambitious through route never came to fruition.

Pending any progress with the Upper Severn scheme, then, LINCOMB LOCK is the highest on the Severn. It lies in a picturesque setting dominated by one of the sheer red sandstone cliffs which characterise the river in this part of the world. There is another such dramatic outcrop between Lincomb and Stourport known as Redstone Lock, a refuge, apparently, of outlaws in Cromwell's time. Opposite the rock, an oil depot and well piled wharf mark the destination of the Severn's last commercial traffics above Worcester, an activity which ceased, sadly, in the 1960s.

The Canal

Secretive, might be the best way to describe the Staffordshire & Worcestershire Canal's approach to (and departure from) its southern terminus at Stourport. Though sharing a wide enough valley with the Stour, the canal tends to be masked by trees and vegetation, and as a consequence has something of a reclusive character to it. Boaters not inclined to proceed beyond the confines of the canal are advised to moor above York Street Lock where 5-day visitor moorings are provided opposite the site of the canal company's workshops, recently redeveloped into not unattractive modern housing.

Leaving Stourport by the back door, the canal is soon curving beneath the old railway bridge which carried the Severn Valley Railway between Hartlebury and Bewdley. There used to be a canal/rail interchange dock at this point. Rusty mooring rings set into a high brick retaining wall recall busier times here, and on the towpath side you might spot a roller around which a line would be taken to aid access to and from the tightly-angled loading dock. Another distant echo of bygone trading days is encountered by Bridge 10A, through which a branch canal long ago led down by way of a lock into the River Stour for boats to reach Wilden Ironworks across the valley. Steel from South Wales and coal from Highley mine, north of Bewdley, would be transhipped at the aforementioned railway basin and taken the short distance to the ironworks by boat. It would be good to turn a bend and encounter such trade now instead of listening to the constant drone of lorries on the Stourport-Kidderminster road.

Kidderminster Lock, Staffordshire & Worcestershire Canal

THE carpet-making town of Kidderminster was in the throes of redevelopment as we researched the sixth edition of this guide; all the usual suspects: fast-food outlets, supermarkets, ring roads and retail parks. Yet one or two of the old carpet factories remain intact, putting up with, if not exactly enjoying, new 21st century uses.

South of the town two isolated locks, couched in the shadow of sandstone outcrops, are separated by a high viaduct over which steam trains of the Severn Valley Railway puff and pant their way between Kidderminster and Bridgnorth; a worthwhile excursion ashore for boaters who have time to spare.

Passing through the centre of town, the canal used to penetrate a deep canyon of factory premises, but these have been demolished, along with another carpet works which once stood above Kidderminster Lock. Now two supermarkets vie for boating custom and provide good moorings in the process, but personally we still prefer (during daytime at least) those at the old town wharf (on the offside above the lock) which are handsomely overlooked by the imposing parish church.

North of Kidderminster, the canal quickly establishes its more obvious rural charms. Wolverley Court Lock lies in a seemingly remote parcel of scrubland in an area once extensively used for sand extraction. Wolverley Lock is overlooked by a quaint pub, the village itself (pretty and worth visiting) lying about ten minutes walk to the west. North of here, delving into glades of balsam and convolvulus, bluebells and foxgloves, the canal is at its most beguilingly attractive. You grow to wish it would go on for ever.

Until relatively recently the Elan Valley water pipe-line used to cross the canal between bridges 21 and 22, now it is culverted beneath it. Completed in 1907, this 73 mile pipe brings water from reservoirs in the Rhayader Mountains of Wales to the bathtubs of Birmingham and the Black Country. The pipe-line's construction at the turn of the century was a huge undertaking, and one of the last great adventures of the 'navvies': "rough, violent men, whose speech had foreign inflections and whose corduroys were caked with the mud of four counties," wrote Francis Brett Young in the preface to one of his most enjoyable novels, *House Under the Water* inspired by the project.

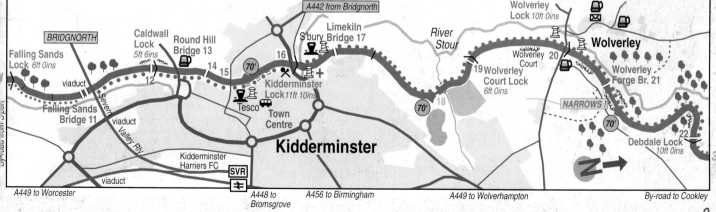

IS there a prettier length of canal in the country? Rivals spring to mind, but none lovelier than the Staffs & Worcs, winding its wooded way from Cookley to Stourton past Kinver with its church perched high on Kinver Edge. There is a "Toytown" ambience about this whole canal which the Swiss would thoroughly approve of. Arguably the prettiest length of all lies between Hyde Lock and Dunsley's diminutive tunnel. Here, bordered by woods on one side, the canal glides past meadows backed by a conifer plantation. It would be difficult to imagine a more rural scene, yet a huge ironworks stood in the vicinity for two centuries. In its heyday twenty puddling furnaces produced wrought iron and the premises lined the canal for some distance. But only the manager's house remains, demurely situated beside the towpath above Hyde Lock. One is awestruck that such a massive undertaking can vanish so completely, until the realisation comes that the same process of change and renewal is taking place throughout the neighbouring Black Country, as the traditional heavy industries of the region are replaced by urban forests and shopping malls.

Barely had the ironworks' pandemonium ceased, when a new interloper arrived on the Stour Valley scene, in the shape of a curious little narrow gauge railway operated with electric trams. The Kinver Light Railway opened in 1901 and lasted only twenty-nine years, but in its short existence brought thousands of day-trippers from the Black Country to Kinver, flaunted by the operating company as the "Switzerland of the Midlands". On Whit Monday, 1905, nearly seventeen thousand passengers were carried along the five mile line from Amblecote, near Stourbridge. The 3ft 6ins gauge track (along which through cars ran from as far away

Kinver Edge

Kinver

The Vine

Hyde Lock 10ft 0ins

site of old ironworks

Dunsley Hall

Course of Kinver Light Rly.

Stourton Castle

waterworks

Devil's Den

Kinver Lock 7ft 3ins

Anchor Hotel

Whittington Lock 9ft 9ins

Whittington Horse Br. 28

70'

Stewponey Lock 10ft

31A 32

gifts

STOURTON JUNCTION

Stour Aq'duct

70'

33

DUNSLEY TUNNEL 25 yards

R. Stour

COOKLEY TUNNEL 65 yards

ironworks

Worcestershire

Cookley

Rock Tavern

The Anchor

Austcliff Bridge 24

Caunsall Bridge 26

Clay House Br. 25

Staffordshire

Stourton Locks 36ft 3ins

Stourton

70'

A449 from Kidderminster

A449 to Wolverhampton

The towpath is in generally good condition, and used by walkers and cyclists alike. Short walks abound in the vicinity of Kinver where good car parking is available or you can use the bus from Stourbridge and walk back via Stourton Junction.

*Figures refer to Staffs & Worcs route.

as Birmingham) crossed the canal at Stewponey, ran alongside it at Hyde, and terminated at Mill Lane, Kinver where the pumping station now stands.

STEWPONEY was a focal point for boat traffic on the Staffs & Worcs. Facilities included a wharf, stables, toll office, workshop and employees' cottages. The former toll house is now home to a gift shop run by Paul De'Aaran, 'international clairvoyant' - Tel: 01384 877110. Presumably he'll be only too happy to tell you what next year's stoppage list contains. Even after the Second World War, in excess of fifty boat loads of Cannock Chase and Baggeridge Colliery coal was being worked through here to Stourport Power Station each week. But in 1949 the National Coal Board announced a florin surcharge on each ton of coal loaded on to boats. Not entirely surprisingly, the traffic rapidly transferred to rail. A few years of desultory day boat trading to Swindon Steel works, 'railway' boats off the Stourbridge Canal, and occasional cargoes of baled wool to Stourport from 'up north' followed, and then, without anyone really noticing, the working boats were gone.

Stewponey doesn't find its way on to Ordnance Survey maps, but is a name of local currency, thought to be derived from an old soldier, returning with a Spanish wife from the town of Estepona, who opened an inn here, the name of which was soon corrupted by Black Country vowels. The inn was rebuilt as a roadhouse in the Thirties, one of those huge joints which were honeypots in the early days of motoring when there was still an element of romance to be found on the roads; there was even a lido in the grounds at one time. Architecturally it had a good deal going for it, even in the debased years of its decline, so it is sad to discover that it has been demolished and replaced by housing completely devoid of any aesthetic ambition. Sometimes you wonder just how such schemes get past their planning application don't you!

At STOURTON JUNCTION four chambers raise the Stourbridge Canal up on its way to the Black Country. Canal junctions don't come much more attractive than this and, even if your itinerary commits you to the Staffs & Worcs, you could do worse than spend a night in Stourbridge, little more than an hour and a half away as described on Map 33.

North of Stourton Junction, the canal - known colloquially as the 'Stour Cut' - bridges the river of the same name. The setting is idyllic, the river tumbling over a shallow weir just upstream of the double-arch aqueduct, and issuing from the adjoining bend, a broad pool. Close by, a peculiar cave is cut out of the rocks at water level. Known as "Devil's Den", it is thought to have been used as a boathouse by the Foley family of Prestwood Hall.

Southwards from Stewponey, the river is the canal's constant companion, the man made waterway keeping pace with the Stour's gradual descent to the Severn by way of occasional, isolated locks of great charm. It is difficult to think of another canal bounded by so many trees, their presence broken only by occasional outcrops of Triassic rock. The most dramatic of these - a real cliffhanger! - is near Caunsall where the Bunter pebble beds of Austcliff Rock loom over a bend in the canal. Little less spectacular is the canal's burrowing beneath the old iron-making village of COOKLEY, its houses seemingly precariously poised over the northern portal of Cookley Tunnel.

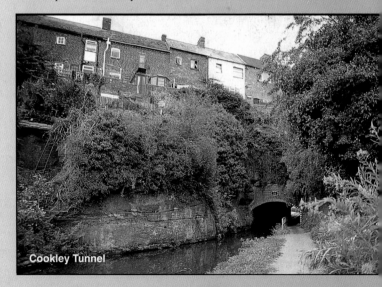

Cookley Tunnel

THE countryside empties. Wales is only the width of an Ordnance Survey map away. These are the landscapes of Francis Brett Young, a writer recently rediscovered by paperback publishers, though still easily found on the shelves of secondhand bookshops. No-one has ever written better about the area between the Black Country and the Welsh Marches. You should try *Far Forest* or *Dr Bradley Remembers*; either would make admirable reading before 'lights out' on your cruise.

Smestow Brook, a tributary of the Stour, is now the canal's chief confidant and friend. In the woods below GOTHERSLEY LOCK stood a canal company roundhouse, a twin to that at Gailey (Map 31) now restored and used as a canalside shop. Both roundhouses date from the year of Trafalgar. The Gothersley one marks the site of an important canal wharf provided to serve a sizeable ironworks which existed here until the 1880s. The roundhouse itself, a gaunt ruin for many years, was storm damaged in 1991 and its base is now the focal point of a picnic site. The ironworks has vanished as well, its forges, furnaces, tramways and wharves superseded by ivy, ash, balsam and butterbur.

GREENSFORGE is a delightful mooring place. Its name recalls the existence of another vanished forge, one which became a mill, the big, four square building of which remains intact and glimpsed through the

alders and willows lining the Smestow. Stroll down the lane and you'll discover its macey, long dry mill pond, an obvious declivity in the reed beds. Nearby an arm extends into ASHWOOD BASIN, now a marina but once an important interchange basin with the Kingswinford Railway, a colliery line dating from 1829 whose first locomotive, *Agenoria*, is now in the National Railway Museum's collection in York.

Between Greensforge and Hinksford locks the canal is bordered by the contrasting images of woodland and a huge static caravan park. Hinksford Pumping Station is one of several waterworks in this part of the valley. Yet another ironworks lined the canal at SWINDON. This one survived until as recently as the early 1970s. Not that you would credit it now, the site being covered - not by flora and fauna - but by the neat lawns, barbecues and conservatory extensions of modern housing. The works was owned at one time by the Baldwin family, of which Stanley became prime minister. Note how the towpath briefly changes sides so that it did not run through the works' precincts. Railway boats traded here with steel blooms from Stourbridge Basin.

BOTTERHAM LOCKS are a staircase pair, so remember to ensure that the top chamber is full and the bottom empty to start with. They raise or lower the canal over twenty feet. North of here the canal becomes temporarily embroiled with the industrial fringe of Wombourne.

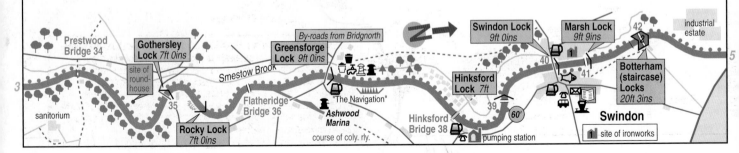

BELOW Bratch the canal skirts Wombourne, skirmishing with industry. The red scars of former sand quarries abound. Narrowboats carried sand from local wharves to Black Country forges for mould making in the casting process.

Bumble Hole and Bratch sound like Dickensian characters. The latter form the canal's best known locks, a trio originally built by Brindley as a staircase, but later separated and provided with extended side pounds to eliminate water waste and traffic delays. Motorised visitors to Bratch have their own car park and picnic site but, apart from a limited length of offside moorings at the foot of the flight, visitor moorings have been sacrificed for a long line of permit-holder moorings to the north of the top lock. As well as the hugely picturesque juxtaposition of the three locks, the Bratch's other attractions include a Victorian pumping station (occasionally open to the public) and a dismantled railway converted into a bridleway and public footpath. The waterworks opened in 1896, its architectural

style being flamboyantly Gothic. Steam engines were used to pump the water until around 1960. Coal to fuel them came in by narrowboat.

The Kingswinford Railway Walk occupies the trackbed of an old Great Western Railway line opened as late as 1925. Passenger trains lasted only seven years, but the station building at Wombourne (less than half a mile east of Bratch Locks) remains intact and is used as a tea room. Wombourne village, whose delightful green lies about a mile to the east, is worth seeking out if you have the time.

North of Bratch the countryside is open and attractively rolling and there are glimpses westwards of the Clee Hills. Working narrowboats are often to be seen moored at Dimmingsdale Wharf. The huge Art Deco style pumping station which was a landmark here for many years has been demolished. There's a pleasant CAMRA recommended country pub called the "Holly Bush" less than a mile to the west of Bridge 53.

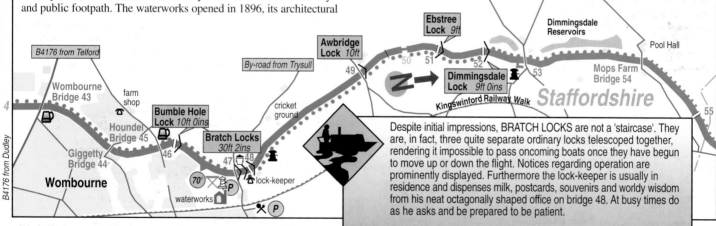

Despite initial impressions, BRATCH LOCKS are not a 'staircase'. They are, in fact, three quite separate ordinary locks telescoped together, rendering it impossible to pass oncoming boats once they have begun to move up or down the flight. Notices regarding operation are prominently displayed. Furthermore the lock-keeper is usually in residence and dispenses milk, postcards, souvenirs and worldy wisdom from his neat octagonally shaped office on bridge 48. At busy times do as he asks and be prepared to be patient.

WOLVERHAMPTON'S western suburbs are what estate agents would term 'residentially desirable' and they harbour little hint of Black Country industry. Moreover, the canal closets itself away from the most pressing overtures of urbanisation, masquerading its way through wooded cuttings to and from a conspirators' assignation with the Birmingham Canal Navigations at Aldersley Junction (Map 7).

If it's a Thursday or Saturday afternoon, make time to stop at WIGHTWICK and visit the nearby manor, no feudal home of a local squire, but a late Victorian mansion which has been in National Trust hands for about fifty years. If you subscribed to the theory that all Victorian architecture was stuffy and overbearing, this lovely house, dating from 1887, may well revise your preconceptions. The interiors were furnished by William Morris and the walls are adorned with Pre-Raphaelite paintings. The grounds are gorgeous too, and there's a working pottery - Tel: 01902 761400.

Evidence suggests that COMPTON LOCK was James Brindley's very first essay in narrow lock construction. It was rebuilt in 1986 and it is interesting to note that the top gate came from Bradley Workshops on the BCN, whilst the bottom pair were provided by British Waterways' depot at Northwich in Cheshire. The chamber is graced by one of the Staffordshire & Worcestershire Canal Society's charming

wooden name posts. The lock also boasts one of the distinctive circular weirs peculiar to this canal.

An impressive girder bridge carries the trackbed of the Wombourne branch railway (now a well-surfaced public right of way) over the canal on the outskirts of Tettenhall. Another old railway bridge of interest remains intact immediately north of Bridge 62A. It carried a private line into Courtaulds' now demolished rayon factory which was also served by Cowburn & Cowpar chemical boats, trading to the adjoining wharf now occupied by a community centre. Another significant canal crossing sees Bridge 62 take Telford's Holyhead Road. In this age of specialisation and anonymity, one can only marvel at one man's contribution to so many aspects of civil and industrial engineering. In the early years of the 19th century, communications between London and Dublin were appalling. Over twenty quite autonomous turnpike trusts were responsible for the road from London via Shrewsbury to Holyhead, the port for Ireland. Yet despite vociferous protests from travellers and the frequent failure of the Mail Coach to penetrate the wilds of Wales at all, matters were not brought to a head until the Act of Union between Britain and Ireland required the regular presence of Irish Members of Parliament at Westminster. Thomas Telford was invited to survey the route and plan improvements, which he did with characteristic thoroughness; recommending widening, resurfacing and numerous gradient modifications, as at the cutting through Tettenhall Rock. Telford's new road opened throughout with the completion of his famous bridge over Menai Strait to Anglesey in 1826.

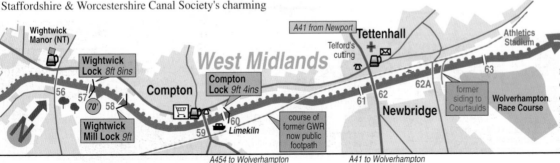

BRINDLEY'S Birmingham Canal of 1772 encounters the proud and ancient manufacturing town of Wolverhampton. North of the town centre the canal negotiates a memorable flight of locks known colloquially as 'The Twenty-one'. At its foot lies an unexpectedly rural junction with the Staffordshire & Worcestershire Canal at ALDERSLEY. There is so much to see that the flight never becomes tedious. The 'Twenty-one' is well maintained and seems somehow less exhausting than one might expect. Brindley only provided twenty chambers, but the last was so deep that it caused water shortages. In 1784 the bottom lock was therefore reduced in depth and a short cutting excavated to carry the canal to a new lock built in the intervening pound. This extra lock - No.20 - gives its identity away by having only one bottom gate.

In working boat days the locks were the haunt of 'hoblers', men or boys who would help single-handed captains through the locks for a small consideration. Another feature of the flight were boat children apparently in the habit of riding horses bareback, at breakneck speed down to Aldersley to collect upcoming boats. Galloping equines are still encountered on the flight in the slightly different shape of racehorses on the neighbouring course; an almost unique juxtaposition - one can only think of Aintree on the Leeds & Liverpool in comparison.

A new Science Park borders the canal between locks 15 to 12 where Clayton tar boats used to ply to and from the gas works. Wolverhampton has always been a fascinating railway centre, and the once rival lines of the Great Western and London Midland & Scottish railways span the canal at several points, notably on a pair of fine viaducts. Lock 11 must have been a trainspotter's idea of heaven when the best of Swindon and Crewe puffed imperiously overhead.

Wolverhampton's refuse incinerator overlooks the middle of the flight. Less conspicuous, but worth looking out for on the towpath side, is the handsome, yet sadly mothballed, Springfield Brewery. Above the top lock - with its picturesque pair of BCN cottages - the canal widens into a landscaped area where handy visitor moorings are provided for overnight stops. The present Broad Street bridge replaces an earlier structure that had cast-iron balustrades and ornate gas lamps and which now graces the Black Country Museum. The adjoining warehouse (recently used, somewhat bizarrely, by Wolverhampton's bright young things as a nightclub) was owned by the famous canal carriers, Fellows, Morton & Clayton.

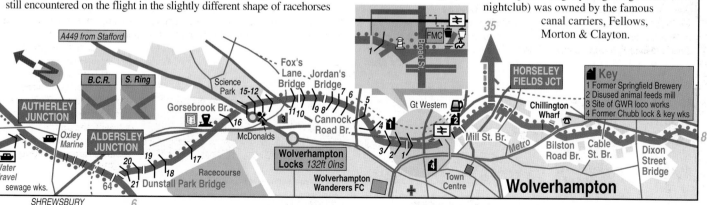

Key
1 Former Springfield Brewery
2 Disused animal feeds mill
3 Site of GWR loco works
4 Former Chubb lock & key wks

Water, Elsan and refuse disposal facilities are obtainable by entering a short arm spanned by a cast iron bridge immediately south of Broad Street Bridge. Like a sizeable wedge of chocolate cake, Chubb's former lock-making works dominates the horizon at this point. This arm was the original course of the canal before it was diverted through Wolverhampton Tunnel when the High Level railway station was built in 1850. Above the tunnel there's a multi-storey car park for rail users. It is said that Wolverhampton's 'ladies of the night' were in the habit of entertaining their customers in the twilight of the canal tunnel.

The canal proceeds through a canyon of largely abandoned industrial buildings to Horseley Fields and the junction of the Wyrley & Essington Canal route to Walsall. There were so many wharves and arms and basins in the vicinity that it would be impractical to go into them here. The emerging railways quickly grasped that development of short haul traffic, to and from the numerous works firmly established beside the densely knit canals, was in their best interest. One, of what amounted to over forty, railway owned basins, remains in surprisingly good condition at Chillington Wharf and has been given Grade II listed status. It was opened by the London & North Western Railway in 1902 on the site of an ironworks, and retains a marked degree of atmosphere in that railway wagons are occasionally stabled on the tracks which flank the still watered canal arm.

South of Wolverhampton the BCN's main line pursues a winding course through a largely industrial area. Bilston Road Bridge carries the Metro tramway across the canal, and there is barely a dull moment as each bend in the canal intrudes upon a fresh variation on the Black Country theme of 'metal bashing'. At Rough Hills Stop the canal narrows at the site of a former toll house.

The Wolverhampton 21

S O what do you think of it so far? - the BCN that is. Are you under its spell, or are you under psychoanalysis, still hyperventilating from its fulminating blend of inspirational industrial heritage and sheer downright ugliness?

Love it, or loathe it, you're here now, so make the most of the BCN's Main Line as, between Wolverhampton and Tipton, in sinuous accord with the contours, it betrays its Brindley origins. Only on the cut through Coseley - engineered by Thomas Telford to by-pass the circuitous Wednesbury Oak Loop (partially retained to serve the maintenance workshops at Bradley) - do 19th century improvements deviate from the original route

of 1772. And if you are prepared to use your imagination, there will barely be a dull moment as the canal traverses an area of the Black Country where the traditional activities of the region are in retreat, their place taken by ubiquitous industrial units and innocuous housing estates. You are a symptom of this change. The relative popularity of boating and walking the BCN is largely a recent phenomenon, helped no little, in the former case, by the popularity of the "Stourport Ring". The recreational potential of canals, however, was recognised too late to save approximately one third of the BCN system from being abandoned during the Fifties and Sixties. Traces of these lost routes abound on this map, and it is difficult not to regret their going, and in doing so daydream of itineraries impossible to recapture afloat, if not on foot.

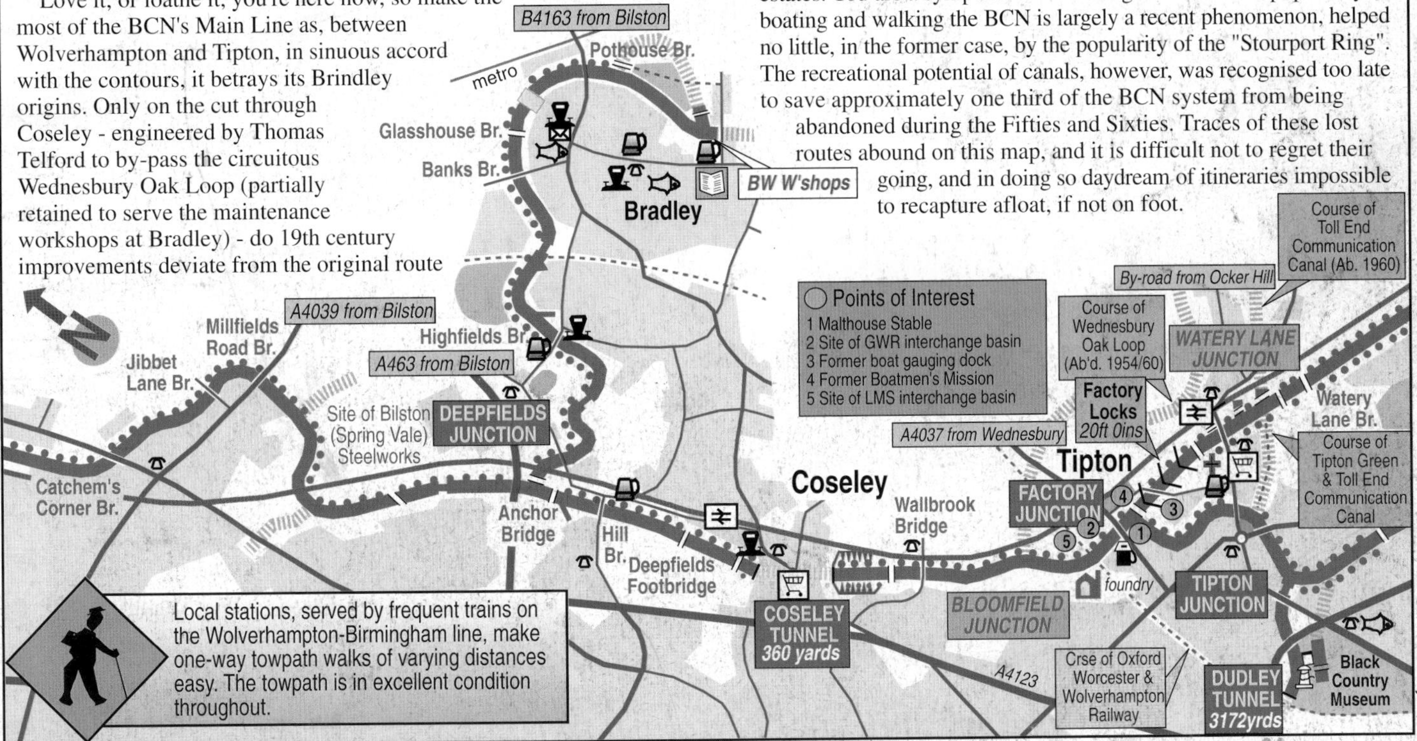

B4163 from Bilston
Pothouse Br.
metro
Glasshouse Br.
Banks Br.
BW W'shops
Bradley

A4039 from Bilston
Millfields Road Br.
Highfields Br.
A463 from Bilston
Jibbet Lane Br.
Site of Bilston (Spring Vale) Steelworks
DEEPFIELDS JUNCTION
Catchem's Corner Br.
Anchor Bridge
Hill Br.
Deepfields Footbridge
Coseley
Wallbrook Bridge
A4037 from Wednesbury

○ Points of Interest
1 Malthouse Stable
2 Site of GWR interchange basin
3 Former boat gauging dock
4 Former Boatmen's Mission
5 Site of LMS interchange basin

Course of Toll End Communication Canal (Ab. 1960)
By-road from Ocker Hill
Course of Wednesbury Oak Loop (Ab'd. 1954/60)
WATERY LANE JUNCTION
Watery Lane Br.
Factory Locks 20ft 0ins
Course of Tipton Green & Toll End Communication Canal
Tipton
FACTORY JUNCTION
TIPTON JUNCTION
foundry
BLOOMFIELD JUNCTION
Crse of Oxford Worcester & Wolverhampton Railway
DUDLEY TUNNEL 3172yrds
Black Country Museum
9a
9b
A4123 Dudley

COSELEY TUNNEL 360 yards

Local stations, served by frequent trains on the Wolverhampton-Birmingham line, make one-way towpath walks of varying distances easy. The towpath is in excellent condition throughout.

*No locks on Old Main Line route

A463 to Sedgley
A4123
A457 to Sedgley
34

Deepfields Junction, BCN Main Line

Utilitarian nomenclature abounds on the BCN, and at FACTORY JUNCTION, Brindley's "Wolverhampton Level" and Telford's "Birmingham Level" are seen to meet or divide, depending on your direction of travel. Boating towards Birmingham you have a choice (always assuming both routes are free of stoppages) between the directness of Telford's wide, embanked, twin-towpathed 'Island Line', twenty feet below through the three Factory Locks, and Brindley's original route which parallels it, hugging the 473ft contour in the shadow of the Rowley Hills. The latter affords access to the BLACK COUNTRY MUSEUM, where secure overnight moorings are available in the surreal environs of a 19th century time warp. Incorporated into the museum, an unusual vertical lift bridge, rescued from the Great Western Railway's Tipton interchange basin (2), gives access to a section of Lord Ward's Canal which led directly from the Old Main Line to a bank of lime kilns which still forms an attractive feature of the museum. Several historic boats are usually on display here, and there is a working boat dock where visitors can see some of the trades and techniques of Black Country boat construction taking place. Beyond the museum moorings is the northern portal of DUDLEY TUNNEL, first dug in 1775 to gain access to subterranean limestone workings. Ten years later it was extended through to join up with the Dudley Canal at PARKHEAD (Map 34). The sole preserve of electrically-powered trip boats for many years, Dudley Tunnel re-opened to general boating traffic in 1992, with the proviso that they be shafted and 'legged' through so as to avoid the creation of engine fumes, and that they meet the fairly restrictive gauge limitations. Life has been made easier by the introduction of a tug to haul you through: contact the Dudley Canal Trust on 01384 236275 for more details.

TIPTON, once waggishly known as the Venice of the Midlands, is rich in canal heritage, and a short circular walk based on the railway station, and incorporating the public footpath now occupying the course of the Tipton Green & Toll End Communication Canal, would provide an immediate, if not intimate, introduction. By FACTORY JUNCTION (named after a long vanished soap works) two interesting buildings survive. Between the pub and the top lock stood a Boatmen's Mission (4), one of five such establishments on the BCN dispensing hot drinks, tobacco, washing facilities and a little transitory warmth and companionship. On the Sabbath the emphasis became more overtly religious, and Sunday School lessons were held for boat children. On the opposite bank of the top lock stands a former BCN gauging station (3) where the carrying capacity of boats was calculated for toll taking purposes. Craft gained access through two arches at the west end of the building. Beyond the junction, in the direction of Wolverhampton and on the far side of the modern road bridge, lay the entrance to the aforementioned Great Western Railway basin (2). Railway owned boats would operate between these interchange points and 'boatage' depots which were wharves operated by the railways but without direct rail links. The London & North Western Railway also had an extensive interchange basin at nearby Bloomfield (5). Back at the junction, alongside the Old Main Line's route, former malthouse stables (1) have been given a new lease of life as a canoe centre - boaters should proceed with due care. Secure overnight moorings are provided here. Snaking round the corner, past "The Fountain" public house and under Owen Street Bridge, Brindley's route skirts the centre of Tipton, passing a small park where the local authority have erected a statue to Tipton's most famous son, the boxer, William Perry, aka 'the Tipton Slasher'! Opposite here, a fairly easily come upon pathway leads between houses along the course of the Communication Canal back to Telford's canal and the railway station. More to the BCN than you thought? You bet!

The Wednesbury Oak Loop

The new route opened in 1837 between Deepfields and Bloomfield junctions was just over a mile long, yet it replaced something like four miles of typical Brindley wanderings which then became known as the Wednesbury Oak Loop. Largely abandoned by 1960, a mile and a half remains in use from Deepfields, a slender channel encroached by floating weed, connecting British Waterways' Bradley Workshop with the main line, a tempting diversion for those - like us - enamoured of the system's byways and backwaters. From the outset a real sense of exploration is engendered as the branch snakes between wastegrounds, its margins reedy, its water turquoise coloured. Tethered ponies dolefully regard your passing. Beyond Sankey's vending machine works there's a glimpse of Bilston's white towered church. In many respects the end comes too soon.

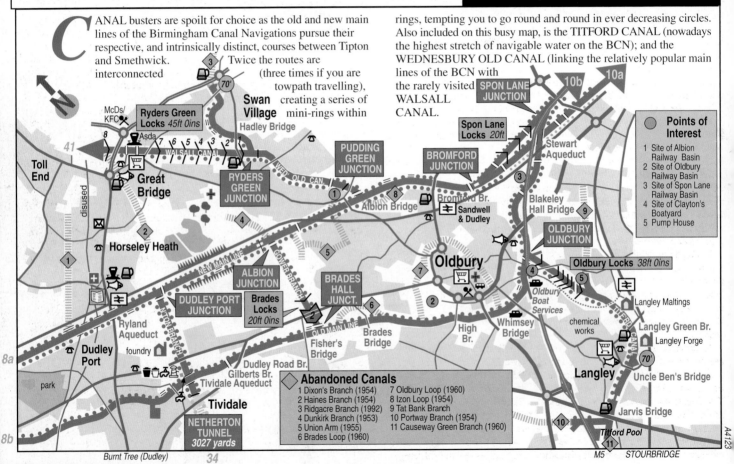

Canal busters are spoilt for choice as the old and new main lines of the Birmingham Canal Navigations pursue their respective, and intrinsically distinct, courses between Tipton and Smethwick. interconnected Twice the routes are (three times if you are towpath travelling), creating a series of mini-rings within rings, tempting you to go round and round in ever decreasing circles. Also included on this busy map, is the TITFORD CANAL (nowadays the highest stretch of navigable water on the BCN); and the WEDNESBURY OLD CANAL (linking the relatively popular main lines of the BCN with the rarely visited WALSALL CANAL.

Points of Interest
1 Site of Albion Railway Basin
2 Site of Oldbury Railway Basin
3 Site of Spon Lane Railway Basin
4 Site of Clayton's Boatyard
5 Pump House

Abandoned Canals
1 Dixon's Branch (1954)
2 Haines Branch (1954)
3 Ridgacre Branch (1992)
4 Dunkirk Branch (1953)
5 Union Arm (1955)
6 Brades Loop (1960)
7 Oldbury Loop (1960)
8 Izon Loop (1954)
9 Tat Bank Branch
10 Portway Branch (1954)
11 Causeway Green Branch (1960)

Map labels:
Ryders Green Locks 45ft 0ins
Swan Village
Hadley Bridge
Walsall Canal
McDs/KFC
Asda
Great Bridge
Toll End
41
disused
Horseley Heath
RYDERS GREEN JUNCTION
WED'Y OLD CAN'
PUDDING GREEN JUNCTION
Albion Bridge
Bromford Br.
Sandwell & Dudley
BROMFORD JUNCTION
Spon Lane Locks 20ft
SPON LANE JUNCTION
10b 10a
Stewart Aqueduct
Blakeley Hall Bridge
OLDBURY JUNCTION
Oldbury
Oldbury Locks 38ft 0ins
Langley Maltings
Langley Green Br.
Langley Forge
70'
Langley
Uncle Ben's Bridge
Whimsey Bridge
High Br.
chemical works
Oldbury Boat Services
NEW MAIN LINE
COVER BRANCH
ALBION JUNCTION
Brades Locks 20ft 0ins
BRADES HALL JUNCT.
OLD MAIN LINE
Fisher's Bridge
Brades Bridge
DUDLEY PORT JUNCTION
Ryland Aqueduct
foundry
Dudley Port
8a
park
Tividale
Dudley Road Br.
Gilberts Br.
Tividale Aqueduct
NETHERTON TUNNEL 3027 yards
8b
Burnt Tree (Dudley)
34
Jarvis Bridge
Titford Pool
M5 STOURBRIDGE
A4123

The Old Main Line

Brindley's route tends to be less boated than Telford's. Duckweed encroaches on the channel whilst moorhens and coots are confident enough in being undisturbed to build precarious nests midstream. East of Tipton the Old Main Line (aka the Wolverhampton Level) runs through council housing, passes beneath the mothballed South Staffordshire Railway, then finds itself in the much changed environment of 'Tividale Quays', a housing development incorporating a large canal basin, underlining the important role that the BCN is playing in the regeneration and 'greening' of the new Black Country. You need to get yourself down to the reference library and study old, large scale maps of the area to grasp the hive of industry which once existed here. Trace the Wolverhampton Level's route past colliery basins, iron foundry basins and brick-works basins and you begin to gain some conception of the canal's former importance. As detailed as we like our maps to be, there was simply no way that we could do justice to the plethora of arms and basins which once branched off the old main line between Tipton and Oldbury. But cruising along here in the rain on a research cruise, we paid them all silent homage and set the dials on our time machine for 1880.

TIVIDALE AQUEDUCT carries the old main line over the Netherton Tunnel Branch. There is no waterway connection here, but a path links the two levels. It's also worth noting that there's a water tap on the upper level, but that the other boating facilities (rubbish, sewage, and another water point) are located down on the lower level adjacent to a pair of British Waterways employees' cottages numbered 174/5 in the old BCN sequence.

At BRADES HALL JUNCTION the Gower Branch descends through the BCN's solitary 'staircase' lock to join Telford's main line, half a mile to the north. More new housing precedes Oldbury, though there are occasional glimpses south towards the Rowley Hills and Dudley Castle. T & S Element, formerly a well known BCN boat company, operated lorries from their premises overlooking Whimsey Bridge for many years, but now appear to have gone out of business.

Vestiges of the Brades and Oldbury loops - which marked the original, even more convoluted course of Brindley's original route - are discernible to the diligent explorer, but the canal's course through Oldbury now is as blandly neat and as unmemorable as a meal from the adjoining drive-thru. OLDBURY JUNCTION (egress point of the Titford Canal) suffers the indignity of being located beneath the M5 motorway. This was the site (between 1935 and 1966) of a boatyard belonging to another carrying company inseparable from the history of this area's canals. Thomas Clayton specialised in the transport of bulk liquids. With a fleet in excess of eighty boats to maintain, this yard presented a busy scene, a distinctive aspect of which were two mobile slipway shelters which provided some protection from the weather while craft were being repaired. Clayton's best known long distance traffic was the carriage of oil from Ellesmere Port to Shell's depot at Langley Green, a contract which lasted from 1924 until 1955; some of the boats remaining horse-drawn until virtually the end.

Southwards from Oldbury, Clayton boats - with their distinctive decked holds and river names - served the gasworks at Oxford, Banbury, Leamington and Solihull, but the bulk of their trade was of a more localised nature, notably the carriage of gas works bi-products such as tar. Their last cargo - carried aboard the now preserved motor *Stour* - arrived at Midland Tar Distillers, Oldbury from Walsall Gasworks on 31st March, 1966. Faced with diminishing cargoes (brought about largely by the advent of North Sea gas) and the disruption brought about by construction of the elevated section of the M5, Thomas Clayton called it a day as far as canal transport was concerned.

Playing hopscotch with the elevated motorway, the old main line proceeds towards Smethwick. Blakeley Hall Bridge possibly recalls the existence of some long-vanished mansion. The simple, hump-backed character of the bridge contrasts starkly with the overhanging motorway's concrete ceiling. In dramatic sequence, the canal passes beneath the Birmingham-Wolverhampton railway, crosses Telford's route by way of the recently refurbished STEWART AQUEDUCT, and meets Brindley's original route to Wednesbury at SPON LANE JUNCTION. The aqueduct's impact is diluted by the hefty pillars of the motorway towering above it. Interestingly, the iron lattice footbridge immediately south of the railway is numbered as a railway and not canal structure, undoubtedly because it was part of the adjoining interchange basin with the London & North Western Railway.

The New Main Line

Whilst Brindley's canal winds about the foot of the Rowley Hills reciting poetry to itself, Telford's gets to grips with the business of reaching Birmingham in a no nonsense manner which accountants would approve of. For almost three miles the canal runs as true as a line on a balance sheet, crossing great open expanses of wasteground where large craters recall past quarrying and brickmaking. These areas have been designated for development as urban woodland. Inexorably the Black Country is becoming green again, going full circle back to its pre-industrial origins.

Junction after junction - some vanished, some intact - keep the adrenalin flowing. The short Dixon's Branch served the Horseley Iron Works foundry which moved from its earlier site at Tipton in 1865. Three aqueducts carry the canal across two roads and a railway. The most notable, RYLAND AQUEDUCT, is a concrete rebuilding of 1968. A short loop railway once crossed the canal here, used by the 'Dudley Dodger' push & pull train which ran from the town station at Dudley to connect with main line trains at Dudley Port. The rusty tracks of the old South Staffordshire Railway betray its lack of use now, all a far cry from the days when Palethorpe's nearby 'sausage siding' was shunted on a daily basis.

At DUDLEY PORT JUNCTION the Netherton Branch makes a bee-line for its famous tunnel. Opened in 1858 to relieve pressure on the parallel Dudley Tunnel route, it was the last canal tunnel to be built in Britain, going into the record books - at 3027 yards - as the eighth longest. Subsequent closures have rendered it third only (in navigable terms) to Standedge on the Huddersfield Narrow Canal and Blisworth on the Grand Union. Various boating facilities are provided on the lower level at TIVIDALE and this is also, reputedly, a secure spot to moor overnight.

Watching the trains go by, you come to ALBION JUNCTION where the Gower Branch links up with the old main line and 'Wolverhampton Level'. A former toll island all but fills the width of the new main line; an 'eye of the needle' job for nervous steerers. Two more junctions tempt you in quick succession. From PUDDING GREEN the door swings open to the under-boated waters of the 'northern half' of the BCN via Brindley's original Wednesbury Canal (see opposite), whilst at BROMFORD JUNCTION there's a link with the old main line through the trio of Spon Lane Locks. Meanwhile Telford's route keeps to the 'Birmingham Level' and passes beneath the M5 and STEWART AQUEDUCT, entering a vast cutting of blue-brick retaining walls between the railway on one side and what's left of Chance's glassworks on the other. The works was known world-wide in its prime as a manufacturer of, amongst many other things, glass for lighthouses.

Dudley Port Junction

The Wednesbury 'Old' Canal

Pudding Green ought to be the name of some picturesque village snuggled deep in the Sussex Weald. Instead, it's an incongruous gateway to and from the northern waters of the BCN; though we did discover wild poppies and lupins flowering bravely along the towpath yards from the junction itself. But flora and fauna - other than the ubiquitous rosebay willowherb - are otherwise none too conspicuous as the canal winds through an area of metal and chemical works past the site of the old Albion railway basin; the inspiration for an atmospheric night-time interior painting by Brian Collings included as a plate in Tom Foxon's evocative memoirs of a working boatman entitled *No.1*. Reference to the Godfrey Edition Ordnance Survey reprint for Greets Green in 1902 illustrates the layout of Albion Basin and, indeed, the full course of the Wednesbury Old Canal to its present truncated terminus at Swan Bridge. Though not as built upon as now, the canal's course is accompanied by numerous side basins and arms - twenty or more at a rough count - emphasising the canal's vital role in the industrialisation process of an area of once wild heathland.

At RYDERS GREEN JUNCTION the Walsall Canal descends through a flight of eight locks to Great Bridge, a route described in the text accompanying Map 41. Veering to the right, Brindley's original canal carries on for another half mile or so to Swan Bridge, a real backwater, even by BCN standards. We cruised it last, on a hot August Bank Holiday, through a carpet of duckweed, passing bricked-up side-bridges and an enigmatic corrugated-iron clad warehouse overhanging a widening in the canal, until presently we came to an abrupt end where the Black Country Spine Road has controversially - in canal circles at any rate - brought about closure of the canal. Historically the canal continued from here to Swan Bridge Junction where one arm, known as the Balls Hill Branch, wound its way to Hill Top, terminating amidst colliery shafts beside the Holyhead Road. A second arm, called the Ridgacre Branch - trifurcated into the long forgotten Dartmouth, Halford and Jesson extremities. Cosmetically restored, you can still walk along the remains of the rest of the canal grateful that much of the rest of the BCN hasn't suffered the same fate.

The Titford Canal

Arguably the BCN's greatest adventure - especially as far as boaters are concerned, for water supply seems perennially problematical - the Titford Canal packs a good deal of interest into its mile and a half journey from the motorwayed enclave of Oldbury Junction to the duck-filled expanses of Titford Pools.

Half a dozen locks - nicknamed 'The Crow' - lift the Titford up to its 511ft height above sea level, nowadays the BCN's loftiest pound. The chambers have single-leaf gates at both top and tail, and the short intervening pounds feature extended side ponds to increase water capacity. With no reservoir, as such, to feed its summit, the Titford Canal relies largely on precipitation to maintain a navigable depth, although back-pumping is also occasionally resorted to.

The canal's surroundings are overwhelmingly industrial, whilst an acrid smell - part chemical, part burnt offering - seems to hang permanently over the proceedings. A gaunt engine house marks the junction with the old Tat Bank Branch; navigable, with care, as far as the first road bridge. Passing under the Great Western Railway's Langley Green-Oldbury branchline (closed to passengers as long ago as the First World War, though only relatively recently to goods) you reach the Wolverhampton & Dudley Brewery's handsome Langley Maltings; stone-blasted clean since our last visit. The water too, seemed cleaner, as clear as a see-through blouse; though the contents of the canal bed thus revealed were not quite so desirable as the analogy suggests.

Langley Forge continues in business; though the thumping presses of previous visits seem unnaturally silent. A neat little park precedes a length of canal embalmed in suburbia before the junction of the old Portway and Causeway Green branch canals heralds the end of navigation; a rather eldritch, road-noisy terminus if the truth were known. Brave boaters can toy with exploration of the coot-haunted, debris-filled Titford Pools, and twice a year the Coombeswood Canal Trust organise campaigning cruises to increase usage and awareness of the Titford Canal. Anecdotal evidence suggests that others have done so and emerged unscathed; physically if not emotionally.

REALISATION of the impact made by Thomas Telford's new main line comes with exploration of the lengthy loops it superseded. By the end of the 18th century Brindley's canal had become a victim of its own success; water was short and traffic congested. Telford was called in to suggest improvements and discovered 'a canal little better than a crooked ditch'! The original towing path had deteriorated to the extent that horses frequently slid and staggered into the water, tow lines entangled when boats met, and boatmen quarrelled over precedence at locks. The canny Scot devised a bold improvement plan cutting through the Smethwick summit. The work took five years and was completed in 1829. It reduced the distance between Wolverhampton and Birmingham by a third. A local historian found the new route "unsurpassed in stupendous magnificence"!

It is difficult to this day not to be impressed by the puissance of Telford's engineering; though just as easy to be beguiled by Brindley's peregrinations. The old loops retained their local traffics, serving works firmly established along their banks. And so the Oozells Street, Iknield Port and Soho (though not the Cape nor Soho Foundry) loops remain navigable to this day, functioning - as does a greater part of the BCN - as storm drainage channels and linear reservoirs for industry. Included in the itineraries of Birmingham's trip boats, they are worth investigating as dreamy alternatives to the unequivocal, focussed concentration of the new main line.

Westwards from SMETHWICK JUNCTION the old and new main lines forge their separate routes to and from Tipton. The earlier canal ascends through three locks to reach its 473ft summit. Originally its course lay even higher at 491ft, traces of which can be discerned along the embankment above the canal as it proceeds west of Brasshouse Lane Bridge. An even better viewpoint is the footbridge straddling the railway just west of Rolfe Street station.

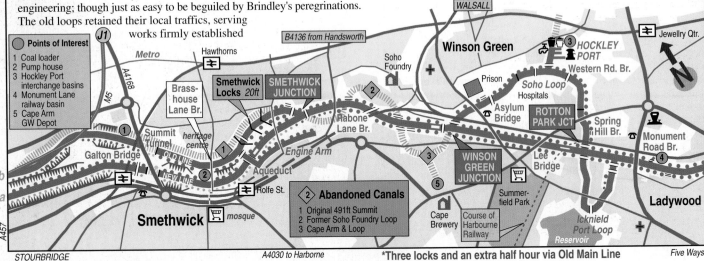

Points of Interest
1 Coal loader
2 Pump house
3 Hockley Port interchange basins
4 Monument Lane railway basin
5 Cape Arm GW Depot

Abandoned Canals
1 Original 491ft Summit
2 Former Soho Foundry Loop
3 Cape Arm & Loop

Three locks and an extra half hour via Old Main Line

From this point there is a grandstand view of the two main lines as they sweep past Smethwick, a scene without equal anywhere else on the inland waterways system; though being Pearsons, and infamously reactionary in outlook, we cannot help but mourn the disappearance of the Brasshouse Lane foundry, transformed, heaven help us, into Wimpey Homes' 'Brindley Village', its honest housing marred by a sequence of hideous descending terraces which would be more at home at West Bromwich Albion's nearby Hawthorns football ground.

Access to the celebrated ENGINE ARM is through the tiny arch of a stone side bridge adjacent to Smethwick Top Lock. The arm spans the new main line by way of a wonderfully Gothic iron bridge, a real treasure in the context of its industrial setting. Unfortunately, as yet, the arm is not equipped with a winding hole, so inquisitive boaters have to back undignifiedly out; but you'll not get them to admit it wasn't worth it. In fact the arm was built to serve as a feeder from Rotton Park Reservoir at Ladywood, and if you scale the grassy bank opposite the junction with the Soho Loop at Winson Green you can see the feeder running through its narrow brick channel. The Engine Arm derives its name from James Watt's 'Smethwick Engine' of 1779 which was introduced to pump water up the original flight of six locks. Even when three of these were by-passed in 1790 the engine continued its work for another century until the pumping engine at Brasshouse Lane was commissioned.

The 1892 pump house has been refurbished by the local authority in conjunction with the adjoining Canal Heritage Centre (see Gazetteer). West of here the old main line, running along the course engineered by Smeaton (of lighthouse fame) penetrates an unexpected oasis of water plantain and rosebay willowherb. For a moment it is possible to make believe you are deep in the countryside, but any rural illusion is shattered by the so-called SUMMIT TUNNEL, an ugly concrete tube covered by the high embankment of a dual carriageway.

Beyond the tunnel the canal is embraced by a deep and swarthy cutting and overlooked by the high rises of West Bromwich. The railway line into Snow Hill crosses the canal adjacent to a derelict concrete structure once used to load boats with coal brought down by cable tramway from the Jubilee Colliery in Sandwell. Odd, isn't it, how a decrepit shell such as this can evoke more sense of the canal's working heyday than many a well meant museum exhibit? A regular run from here was to Kings Norton (Map 12) with coal for the furnaces of the paper mill. The cutting, and any lingering bucolic fancies, come to an abrupt end as the canal is swallowed up beneath the elevated section of the M5.

In contrast with the old line's excursions over the summit, Telford's route lies in shadows cast by extensive earthworks; dank corridors of blue engineering brick retaining walls and precipitous banks of bracken and bramble. The scale of these 19th century works, accomplished by navvies totally without sophisticated machinery, tends to be overwhelming. But the climax is Telford's astonishing GALTON BRIDGE; hidden in both directions by other structures until the last dramatic moment. It has a neighbour in the shape of Galton Bridge station, built as a dual-level interchange between local services on the lines serving Birmingham's New Street and Snow Hill stations.

Between Smethwick and WINSON GREEN the old and new main lines are one, sharing the same route through an industrial heartland of foundries and railway sidings. Much of the fun to be had from exploring the BCN derives from piecing together clues to its past. Railway boats would ease out of the Cape Arm's tunnel like exit with nuts and bolts from GKN destined for the railway basin at HOCKLEY PORT; now a centre for residential moorings. Earlier still, near Rabone Lane Bridge, Matthew Boulton and James Watt opened their Soho foundry, the first factory in the world to be lit by gas so that work could continue after darkness had fallen. Visited by Boswell in 1776, Boulton boasted: 'I sell here, sir, what all the world desires to have - power!' Adjacent to the western junction of the SOHO LOOP (and again beneath the Engine Arm aqueduct) stand the bases of former toll houses. These octagonally shaped offices were strategically sited to keep account of the numerous short-haul traffics which operated throughout the BCN. Now only the bases remain, but a replica has recently been erected at Smethwick Top Lock, so you can judge how interesting these buildings used to be.

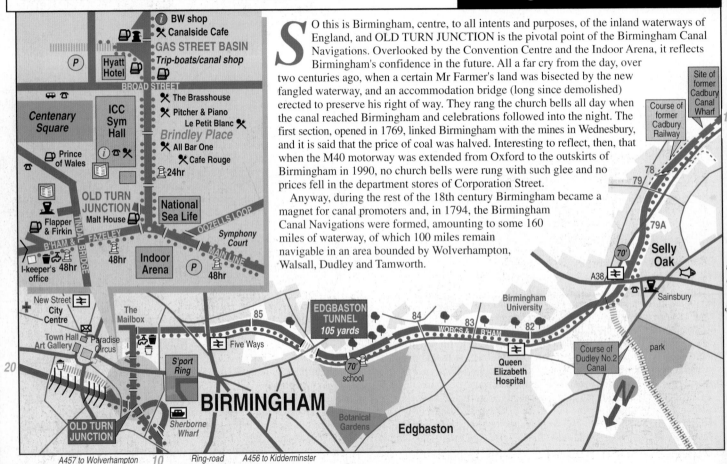

i BW shop
Canalside Cafe
GAS STREET BASIN
Trip-boats/canal shop

P Hyatt Hotel

BROAD STREET

Centenary Square

ICC Sym Hall

Brindley Place

Prince of Wales

OLD TURN JUNCTION
Malt House

National Sea Life

Flapper & Firkin

B'HAM & FAZELEY

TINDAL BRIDGE

l-keeper's office
48hr   48hr   48hr

Indoor Arena
P 48hr

OOZELLS LOOP

MAIN LINE

Symphony Court

The Brasshouse
Pitcher & Piano   Le Petit Blanc
All Bar One
Cafe Rouge
24hr

New Street City Centre

The Mailbox

Town Hall Art Gallery
Paradise Circus

S'port Ring

BIRMINGHAM

Sherborne Wharf

OLD TURN JUNCTION

Five Ways

85

EDGBASTON TUNNEL
105 yards

70'
school

84

Botanical Gardens

Edgbaston

WORCS & B'HAM

83

82

Birmingham University

Queen Elizabeth Hospital

Course of Dudley No.2 Canal

park

Site of former Cadbury Canal Wharf

Course of former Cadbury Railway

78
79

79A

70' Selly Oak

A38   Sainsbury

20

A457 to Wolverhampton   10   Ring-road   A456 to Kidderminster

S O this is Birmingham, centre, to all intents and purposes, of the inland waterways of England, and OLD TURN JUNCTION is the pivotal point of the Birmingham Canal Navigations. Overlooked by the Convention Centre and the Indoor Arena, it reflects Birmingham's confidence in the future. All a far cry from the day, over two centuries ago, when a certain Mr Farmer's land was bisected by the new fangled waterway, and an accommodation bridge (long since demolished) erected to preserve his right of way. They rang the church bells all day when the canal reached Birmingham and celebrations followed into the night. The first section, opened in 1769, linked Birmingham with the mines in Wednesbury, and it is said that the price of coal was halved. Interesting to reflect, then, that when the M40 motorway was extended from Oxford to the outskirts of Birmingham in 1990, no church bells were rung with such glee and no prices fell in the department stores of Corporation Street.

Anyway, during the rest of the 18th century Birmingham became a magnet for canal promoters and, in 1794, the Birmingham Canal Navigations were formed, amounting to some 160 miles of waterway, of which 100 miles remain navigable in an area bounded by Wolverhampton, Walsall, Dudley and Tamworth.

There *were* celebrations, however, in 1991 when the Convention Centre opened alongside the canal, and Birmingham, here, has something to be proud of. Delegates from all over the world are wooed to convene in Birmingham instead of Brussels or Baltimore, and who knows what magic of the BCN might rub off on them: "You mean to say, Elmer, that people actually go boating along those canals for *fun!*"

BRINDLEY PLACE lies at the centre of things now. Here are 24 hour moorings overlooked by a plethora of cafe bars and restaurants - for once the hackneyed analogy of Birmingham with Venice seems almost apt. From the piazzas of the Convention Centre the canal leads through Broad Street tunnel to GAS STREET BASIN, the epitome - and for many the soul - of Birmingham's waterways.

In fact Gas Street had come to symbolise the BCN to such an extent that it was often forgotten that the actual terminal wharf and offices of the Birmingham Canal lay to the east of here. Two arms terminated at the rear of the BCN company's handsomely symmetrical offices on Suffolk Street which, sadly, were demolished in 1928. Demolition controversially took its toll of the Gas Street canalscape in 1975 as well, by which time the planners should have known better, and British Waterways have never really been forgiven for razing their rich heritage of 18th century waterside warehouses to the ground in a calculated move to sidestep a preservation order.

For a time nothing was done to fill the void. Gas Street might have ceased to exist but for a community of residential boats which lent a splash of colour and humanity to a decaying canalscape. A decade elapsed before the developer's proposals were realised in bricks and mortar, and the biggest irony of all is that the new pubs and offices emerged in a warehouse vernacular style of remarkable similarity to the bulldozed originals.

The only post Seventies interloper unsympathetic to the scale of the original Gas Street is the towering, shimmering, slippery, silvered edifice of the Hyatt Hotel. What do its sybaritic guests make of the little boats miles below their air-conditioned eyries? Do they see them as 'local colour', as archaic as the sampans of Hong Kong harbour?

The Worcester & Birmingham Canal

Work began on the Worcester & Birmingham Canal from the Birmingham end in 1794, but it was not until 1815 that the route was completed throughout. Fearful of its water supply disappearing down into the Severn, the Birmingham Canal Company at first refused to be directly linked with the newcomer, and so laborious transhipment of through traffic took place across an infamous divide known as the 'Worcester Bar'. Eventually, however, a stop lock was provided between the two waterways, affording the BCN some measure of protection, yet enabling through passage of boats.

Quickly extracting itself from the wine bars and nightclubs of downtown Birmingham, the Worcester & Birmingham Canal turns right-angle past the new 'Mailbox' development and makes for the sylvan suburbs of Edgbaston. It was this cloistered, arboreous entrance to and exit from the city that prompted Robert Aickman to express the aphorism: "Canals stretch green fingers into towns." He might have added yellow and purple to his palate, for by late summer the borders of the canal and adjoining railway are a riot of rosebay willowherb and golden rod. But we can't help but share his enthusiasm, for this is a lovely stretch of canal, given its proximity to the city centre, and its towpath is increasingly used by walkers and cyclists as an alternative to the choked carriageways of the A38.

In cahoots with the old Birmingham West Suburban Railway, opened in 1876, and now heavily trafficked with sleek green electric units interspersed with Virgin Voyagers, the canal skirts Birmingham University, whose Italianate tower stabs the sky. At SELLY OAK there is little indication left of the junction with the former Dudley No.2 Canal, though west of the A4040 the course of the canal has been turned into a public footpath, virtually as far as the tunnel at Lapal. Journeying southwards, the Worcester & Birmingham reaches the outskirts of the chocolate making centre of Bournville. Again there are scant remains of the canal's heyday, when its east bank was a busy point of interchange for Cadbury's fleet of narrowboats and its internal railway system shunted by its own fleet of perky tank locomotives painted in a dark red colour inspired by the company's cocoa tins.

AT King's Norton the Stratford Canal comes in to join the Worcester & Birmingham, a route described in our "Severn & Avon Companion". North of the junction the Worcester & Birmingham trudges somewhat dolefully through an urban landscape of factory walls and sundry industrial premises, the only surprise being an indoor cricket centre located, more or less, on the site of a former Midland Railway interchange basin. BOURNVILLE railway station lies alongside the canal by Bridge 77. Moorings for Cadbury World (Tel: 0121 451 4180) are located alongside the railway station on the towpath side. Bournville's garden village owes its existence to the altruism of Quakers Richard and George Cadbury who built a chocolate factory on a greenfield site in the vicinity in 1879. The name Bournville dates from that time: Bourn relating to a local watercourse, whilst the rather fanciful suffix

of 'ville' was deemed to have desirable French overtones, more readily marketed than Foundry Lane Chocolate or some similar more realistic and accurate trade mark.

King's Norton Junction retains a handsome junction house and a lucid signpost, but beware being beguiled by the open swards of the adjacent parkland, for the natives are said to be restless in these parts - if not drug-crazed - and at least one major hire fleet operator doesn't encourage boaters to linger in the vicinity. For a number of years the buildings by Bridge 72 housed an historic collection of cars in premises which had once been a paper mill.

WAST HILL TUNNEL is the Worcester & Birmingham's longest. It takes around half an hour to pass through and, whilst appearances can be deceptive, there is room to pass oncoming craft inside its gloomy depths. As your eyes become accustomed to daylight again, you'll notice that the scene shifters have been busy: southbound the delights of

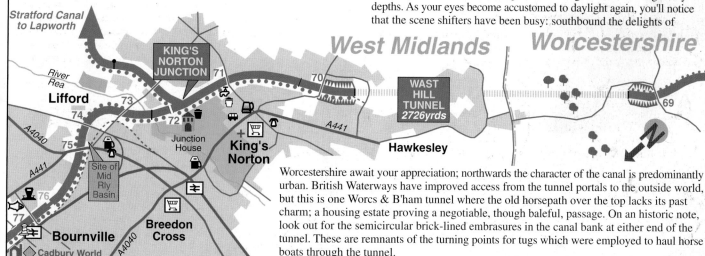

Worcestershire await your appreciation; northwards the character of the canal is predominantly urban. British Waterways have improved access from the tunnel portals to the outside world, but this is one Worcs & B'ham tunnel where the old horsepath over the top lacks its past charm; a housing estate proving a negotiable, though baleful, passage. On an historic note, look out for the semicircular brick-lined embrasures in the canal bank at either end of the tunnel. These are remnants of the turning points for tugs which were employed to haul horse boats through the tunnel.

POST-WAR Alvechurch overspills up its hillside to fringe the canal, but barely deflects it from its dreamy, lock-less progress above the valley of the Arrow. There are panoramic views eastwards towards Weatheroak Hill, crossed by the Romans' Ryknild Street. A feeder comes in from Upper Bittell Reservoir beside an isolated canal employee's cottage near Bridge 66. The Lower Reservoir, rich in wildfowl, lies alongside the canal and is given a gorgeous wooded backdrop by the Lickey Hills. Only the Upper Reservoir feeds the canal. The Lower was provided by the canal company to compensate millers in the vicinity whose water supplies from the River Arrow had been affected by the construction of the canal. In 1985 a short section of the canal was re-routed to accommodate construction of the M42 motorway.

Bridge 62 carries the electrified commuter line from Redditch through Birmingham to Lichfield. A seventy-five minute train journey - three days by boat to the nearest canal settlement at Fradley Junction (Map 25). But time is an irrelevance on the canals, so relax and savour the charms of Shortwood Tunnel, its approach cuttings so suffocated by the odour of wild garlic that you feel as if you are being embraced by an over enthusiastic Frenchman. All that's missing is the tang of Gauloise, but then you may be able to provide that yourself.

As with all other Worcester & Birmingham tunnels (Edgbaston excepted) the towpath isn't subterranean, but the old horse-path across the top remains well-defined, and it is pleasant to wander across the top, fantasising that you've a horse to lead while your boat is hauled through the earth beneath your feet by one of the erstwhile tunnel tugs.

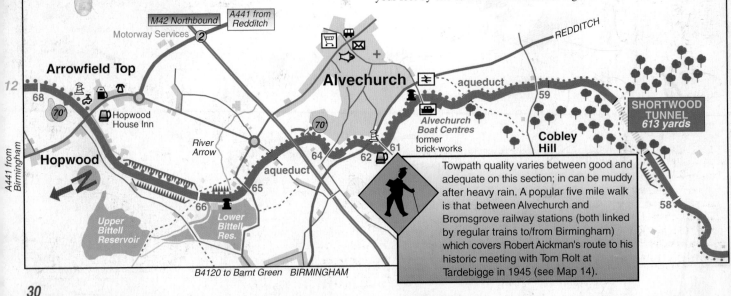

Towpath quality varies between good and adequate on this section; in can be muddy after heavy rain. A popular five mile walk is that between Alvechurch and Bromsgrove railway stations (both linked by regular trains to/from Birmingham) which covers Robert Aickman's route to his historic meeting with Tom Rolt at Tardebigge in 1945 (see Map 14).

TARDEBIGGE represents a boater's Rite of Passage. Once you have tackled this flight which, coupled with the neighbouring six at Stoke, amount to thirty-six locks in four miles, other groups of locks, however fiendish, however formidable, pale into insignificance. The thirty chambers of the Tardebigge flight raise the canal over two hundred feet, the top lock - somewhat removed from the rest - being, at 14 feet, one of the deepest narrowbeam locks on the system; it replaced a lift prone to malfunction and water wastage. Well maintained and surrounded by fine countryside, Tardebigge Locks are there to be enjoyed, not dreaded. In any case you are apt to fall into a hypnotically rhythmic trance as the hours and successive chambers

Waterways Association was formed. A plinth adjacent to the lock tells the story, though it is generally accepted now that the meeting actually took place in 1945 and not a year later as originally recorded.

Only the briefest of pounds separates the Tardebigge and Stoke flights. Room enough, just, for half a dozen boats to moor for an overnight breather adjacent to a popular pub.

The picturesque former lock-keeper's cottage between locks 31 and 32 is now available for let by the admirable Landmark Trust, a body devoted to the rescue and promotion of worthwhile buildings of all shapes and sizes. Indeed, it is said that the demolition of the junction house at Hurlestone on the Shropshire Union Canal 'maddened' the Trust's founder, John Smith, into founding the organisation in 1965. For more details of their work and holiday lets telephone: 01628 825925.

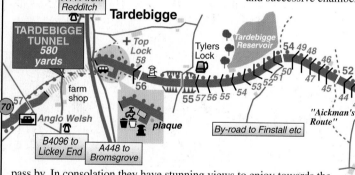

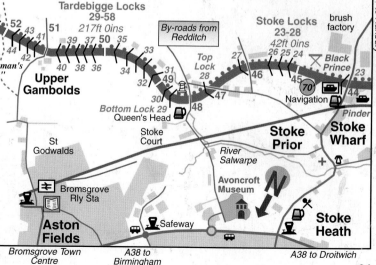

pass by. In consolation they have stunning views to enjoy towards the Malvern Hills and plenty of fellow travellers with which to pass the time of day and share the lock routine.

Tardebigge itself holds a special place in the story of the inland waterways movement. It was to here that Robert Aickman and his wife made their way from Bromsgrove station (at the foot of the Lickey Incline) to meet Tom and Angela Rolt aboard their narrowboat home, *Cressy*, which had been moored above the top lock throughout the Second World War. As a direct result of their meeting the Inland

NOWADAYS, Britain's salt industry is largely confined to Cheshire but, as the name Droitwich suggests, this part of Worcestershire was once a centre of salt making too. The salt obsessed Romans built a special road between Droitwich and Alcester to carry this valuable commodity. Similarly, the Worcester & Birmingham built the short Droitwich Junction Canal from Hanbury Wharf to carry the same cargo. Barely two miles long, it included seven locks and passed briefly into the River Salwarpe before meeting the previously established Droitwich Canal at Vines Park near the town centre. Both the Droitwich canals had lapsed into dereliction before the end of the Thirties. In recent years they have undergone varying degrees of restoration and funding is still being sought to raise the necessary finance to fully reinstate both canals, thus forming a twenty mile cruising ring incorporating the adjoining Worcester & Birmingham Canal and River Severn. The year 2007 has been earmarked as a target for re-opening.

At the end of the 18th century, John Corbett, son of a local boatman, discovered large deposits of brine at Stoke Prior and developed the largest salt works in the world on the site. It made his fortune. He met an Irish woman in Paris, married her and built a replica French chateau for her on the outskirts of Droitwich, a town he transformed from one of industrial squalor into a fashionable spa. In its heyday the canalside works at Stoke was producing 200,000 tons of salt a year. The company had a fleet of narrowboats and hundreds of railway wagons. Corbett died in 1901 and is buried at the pretty little church of St Michael's, Stoke Prior (Map 14). His vast works, later part of ICI, was demolished in the 1970s.

Canal and railway join forces again beside the Astwood flight, drifting lazily through lush farmland overlooked by the wooded slopes of Summer Hill to the east. Westward views encompass Abberley and Woodbury hills beyond the River Severn. Closer at hand are the twin 700ft high masts of Wychbold radio transmitting station. Opened in 1934, its call sign "Droitwich Calling" became known throughout Britain and in many parts of Europe. During the Second World War Droitwich's long range transmitter broadcast the 'voice of freedom' throughout occupied Europe.

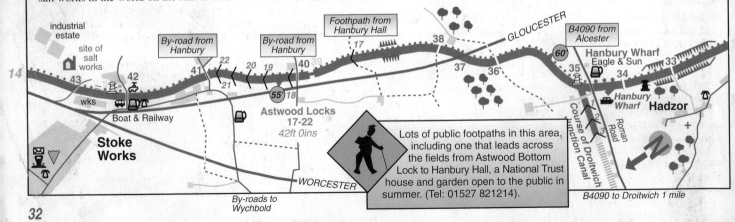

Lots of public footpaths in this area, including one that leads across the fields from Astwood Bottom Lock to Hanbury Hall, a National Trust house and garden open to the public in summer. (Tel: 01527 821214).

THE canal skirts the mellow settlements of Shernal Green, Dunhampstead, Oddingley and Tibberton and, in spite of being sandwiched by the railway and motorway, seems remote and untouched. High clumps of sedge border the canal, swaying with the passage of each boat and somehow emphasising the loneliness of the landscape. Occasionally a by-road crosses the canal, wandering eastwards into an empty tract of countryside which was once part of the Royal Forest of Feckenham.

DUNHAMPSTEAD TUNNEL is tiny compared to the 'big three' to the north, but like them it has no towpath, forcing walkers to take to the old horse-path which threads its way through bosky woodlands above. A small hire fleet base adds traffic to the canal at this point, whilst a craft shop and convivial country pub provide an excuse to break your journey.

ODDINGLEY consists of little more than an ancient half-timbered manor house, a tiny church and a level-crossing keeper's house and cabin: no shops, no pubs, just the reedy canal and the occasional cacophony of a passing train. Tibberton, on the other hand, is a long straggling village of mostly modern housing with a useful (if modestly stocked) post office stores and a pair of pubs. Well piled visitor moorings are provided west of bridge 25.

A deep cutting and the M5 motorway separates Tibberton from OFFERTON LOCKS. Boating northwards you can now take a breather. Southbound the locks begin again as the Worcester & Birmingham completes its descent to the Severn.

Two aspects of this canal's working practice were remarkable. Boats kept left when passing each other and pairs of donkeys were widely used in place of horses to haul the boats. The animals worked well together as long as they 'knew' one another, but the introduction of a new donkey would cause considerable ructions.

One of the last traders on the Worcester & Birmingham Canal was Charles Ballinger of Gloucester. He was still using horse-drawn boats as late as 1954, carrying coal from the Cannock area to Townsend's mill at Diglis. Occasionally he would have an 'uphill' cargo as well: matches from Gloucester to Birmingham, or flour from Worcester to Tipton; but by the beginning of the Sixties trade had deserted the canal.

A4538 from Evesham

M5 Southbound

Tibberton

Business Park

N

6

rugby ground

22A

70'

25

24A

24

17

16

15 14 13 12

23 11

M5 Northbound

26

27 Oddingley

28

Offerton Locks 11-16
42ft 0ins

A4538 to Droitwich

A449 to Worcester

29

70'

The Firs
Forge Studio

30

Brook Line

Dunhampstead

DUNHAMPSTEAD TUNNEL
236 yards

B'HAM

Shernal Green

31

32

15   By-road to Droitwich

33

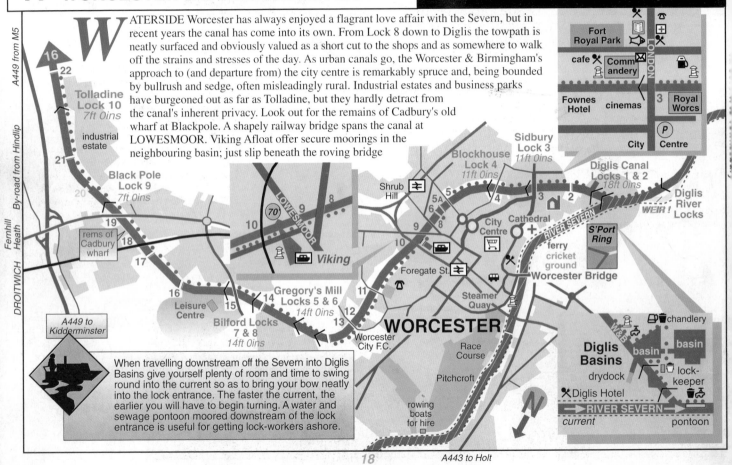

W ATERSIDE Worcester has always enjoyed a flagrant love affair with the Severn, but in recent years the canal has come into its own. From Lock 8 down to Diglis the towpath is neatly surfaced and obviously valued as a short cut to the shops and as somewhere to walk off the strains and stresses of the day. As urban canals go, the Worcester & Birmingham's approach to (and departure from) the city centre is remarkably spruce and, being bounded by bullrush and sedge, often misleadingly rural. Industrial estates and business parks have burgeoned out as far as Tolladine, but they hardly detract from the canal's inherent privacy. Look out for the remains of Cadbury's old wharf at Blackpole. A shapely railway bridge spans the canal at LOWESMOOR. Viking Afloat offer secure moorings in the neighbouring basin; just slip beneath the roving bridge

When travelling downstream off the Severn into Diglis Basins give yourself plenty of room and time to swing round into the current so as to bring your bow neatly into the lock entrance. The faster the current, the earlier you will have to begin turning. A water and sewage pontoon moored downstream of the lock entrance is useful for getting lock-workers ashore.

Tolladine Lock 10 *7ft 0ins*
industrial estate
Black Pole Lock 9 *7ft 0ins*
rems of Cadbury wharf
Leisure Centre
A449 to Kidderminster
Gregory's Mill Locks 5 & 6 *14ft 0ins*
Bilford Locks 7 & 8 *14ft 0ins*
Worcester City F.C.
LOWESMOOR
Viking
Shrub Hill
Blockhouse Lock 4 *11ft 0ins*
Sidbury Lock 3 *11ft 0ins*
City Centre
Cathedral
Foregate St.
WORCESTER
Steamer Quay
Race Course
Pitchcroft
rowing boats for hire
RIVER SEVERN
ferry
cricket ground
Worcester Bridge
S'Port Ring
Diglis Canal Locks 1 & 2 *18ft 0ins*
Diglis River Locks
WEIR!
Fort Royal Park
cafe
Comm andery
Fownes Hotel
cinemas
Royal Worcs
City Centre
chandlery
basin
Diglis Basins
basin
drydock
lock-keeper
Diglis Hotel
RIVER SEVERN
current
pontoon

A449 from M5
By-road from Hindlip
Fernhill Heath
DROITWICH

18
A443 to Holt

and ask permission at the boatyard office. An industrial interlude follows as the canal winds past engineering works. This is followed by an area of terraced streets. By Sidbury Lock stands The Commandery which Charles II used as his headquarters during the Battle of Worcester in 1651, though the building itself was originally a hospital and dates from as early as the 15th century. There is room here for half a dozen or so boats to moor overnight within mellifluous earshot of the Cathedral clock.

Another industrial reach follows as the canal slips past the famous Royal Worcester porcelain works and Townsend's Mill, once intensive users of water transport, both via the river and via the canal.

DIGLIS BASINS were opened in the19th century to facilitate transhipment of cargoes between river and canal. These days they are full of boats familiar with the slap of saltwater on their bottoms. The basins are a great place for wandering inquisitively amidst the smell of paint and tar, the noise of wood being sawn, and metal being bent into shape. Two broad locks separate the basins from the river. They are closed at night and don't open again until around eight in the morning when the lock-keeper comes on duty - Tel: 01905 358758. In most cases he doesn't get involved in operating the locks, but it is good to know that he is about should you need help or advice. Downstream the river heads for Tewkesbury and Gloucester through Diglis River Locks as covered in our *Severn & Avon Canal and River Companion.*

Upstream, 'Sabrina' flows beneath the great west window of the Cathedral, the juxtaposition of the noble building and the wide river being one of the great inland waterway scenes. Antiquated wharves and warehouses line the east bank of the river south of WORCESTER BRIDGE. Widened in the 1930s, the old parapet found its way into Edward Elgar's garden, so enamoured was the composer of anything associated with his home town. On summer weekends a ferry operates in the vicinity of the Cathedral, and trip boats ply this reach as well, so keep a weather eye open for sudden manoeuvres. Limited official moorings are available on the city side between the old road bridge and the ornate, cast iron railway bridge which carries the Malvern and Hereford line across the river. A third bridge spanning the Severn is of modern origin, being a stylish pedestrian link between the city centre and the west bank's suburbs. Passing rowing clubs, and the racecourse, the river traveller heads upstream for more rural locales.

Diglis Basins

THE Malvern Hills come into view in the neighbourhood of Bevere, glimpsed on the south-west horizon behind the spire of Hallow church. Queen Elizabeth I is said to have hunted for deer hereabouts. Another historical figure, albeit a peripheral one, with associations in the area was Napoleon's brother, Lucien Bonaparte, who lived in exile near Grimley for a period of time.

Make the most of your brief encounter with the Severn. For unless you choose to tie up, perhaps - if there is room - at Bevere or Holt locks, or at one of the riparian hostelries, like the "Camp House" - the three or four hours spent on the river between Worcester and Stourport are apt to flash swiftly by, leaving you with just a treasured blur of alder and willow fringed banks broken by occasional outcrops of sandstone; caravan parks and static homes; cattle or anglers flank or thigh high in the river margin; kingfishers skimming like low flying aircraft over the water's surface; and the unruffled routine of the automated locks.

A loop in the river forms the three acre island of Bevere, a place of refuge for the good burghers of Worcester in medieval times when war or plague threatened. Just upstream the little River Salwarpe enters unostentatiously from the east, having risen on the slopes of the Lickey Hills and wound down through Bromsgrove and Droitwich to meet the Severn. Alongside, between two houses mostly hidden by foliage, lie the remains of the bottom lock of the Droitwich Canal. Opened in 1771 and surveyed by Brindley - though actually engineered by John Priddey - the canal flourished during the 19th century as an export route for the salt industry, an activity carried out in the vicinity of Droitwich since Roman times. When salt making declined this 'barge' canal fell into decay and was disused by the First World War, its horse-drawn trows just a memory. In 1973 a trust was formed to restore the canal, and, so far, the summit pound and a sizeable basin in central Droitwich have been returned to water. Further progress must wait until more funding is in place, though 2007 has been pencilled in as a possible date for reopening.

The village of Grimley sits well back from the river, though anglers make use of the bumpy lane down to the water's edge to reach their perches in amongst the musky clumps of balsam. The public footpath which has accompanied the west bank of the Severn all the way up from Worcester ends abruptly opposite Hawford at the site of a long abandoned ferry.

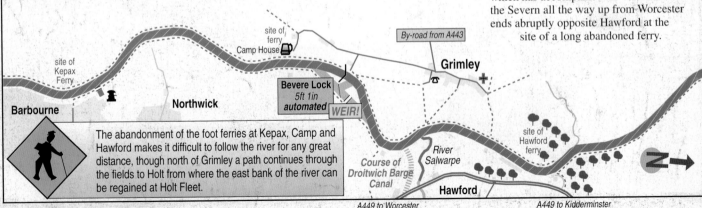

The abandonment of the foot ferries at Kepax, Camp and Hawford makes it difficult to follow the river for any great distance, though north of Grimley a path continues through the fields to Holt from where the east bank of the river can be regained at Holt Fleet.

Bevere Lock on the River Severn

ANYONE so disposed could forget the present in Shrawley Woods," wrote L.T.C. Rolt in his 1949 topographical guide to the county of Worcestershire, going on to evoke two halcyon summer days moored on *Cressy* along this most beautiful of upper navigable Severn reaches between Holt and Lincomb locks. Disregard for the present implies a nostalgia for the past, and it is intriguing to discover that Dick Brook - emerging almost imperceptibly out of the shadowy trees on the west bank of the river - was once made navigable in the 17th century to serve a forge located deep in the woods. Two or three lock chambers were cut out of the sandstone, and barges trading up from the Forest of Dean conveyed cargoes of pig iron along the narrow stream to the doors of the forge.

The Holts provide vestiges of civilisation alongside the river's otherwise remote course: Holt, Holt Heath, Holt Fleet and, just off the edge of our map, Holt Who Goes There? A rash of caravan parks and shanty-like chalets mar otherwise unspoilt riverside meadows for everyone but their proud owners. Luckily this manifestation of mankind's capacity for destroying the very tranquillity he desires is confined to those parts

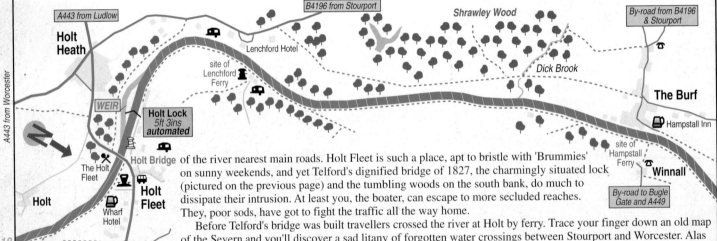

of the river nearest main roads. Holt Fleet is such a place, apt to bristle with 'Brummies' on sunny weekends, and yet Telford's dignified bridge of 1827, the charmingly situated lock (pictured on the previous page) and the tumbling woods on the south bank, do much to dissipate their intrusion. At least you, the boater, can escape to more secluded reaches. They, poor sods, have got to fight the traffic all the way home.

Before Telford's bridge was built travellers crossed the river at Holt by ferry. Trace your finger down an old map of the Severn and you'll discover a sad litany of forgotten water crossings between Stourport and Worcester. Alas the idyllic and (to anyone ever charmed by H.G. Wells' account of 'Mr Polly's' sojourn at the "Potwell Inn") enviable lifestyle of the ferrymen came to an end once people had replaced Sunday afternoon rambles along the riverbank with a drive in a motor car. Not that there wasn't a darker side to ferrying. In 1919 the Hampstall Ferry was swamped by the waves of a passing steamer and sank, drowning nine people.

Black Country Ring

Colwich, Trent & Mersey Canal

WITH twenty-four locks in less than three miles, the BIRMINGHAM & FAZELEY'S departure from (or approach to) Birmingham makes considerable demands on the boater's reservoir of energy: four or five hours hard graft amidst the design studios and tower blocks of the Farmer's Bridge flight and the remorseless redevelopments of "Heartlands". Furthermore, the towpath of the 'Old Thirteen' is such a popular promenade nowadays, that any operation of the locks is likely to be a well-publicised affair, and you are apt to be accompanied, like a tournament golfer, by a crowd of onlookers from chamber to chamber, all inquisitive to know where you've come from and where you're going to and if you're having a good time. Humour them: they've got to get back to their desks and their counters; you have the freedom of 'The Cut'. FARMER'S BRIDGE LOCKS are an object lesson in urban regeneration. They used to be a largely inaccessible, run-down eyesore,

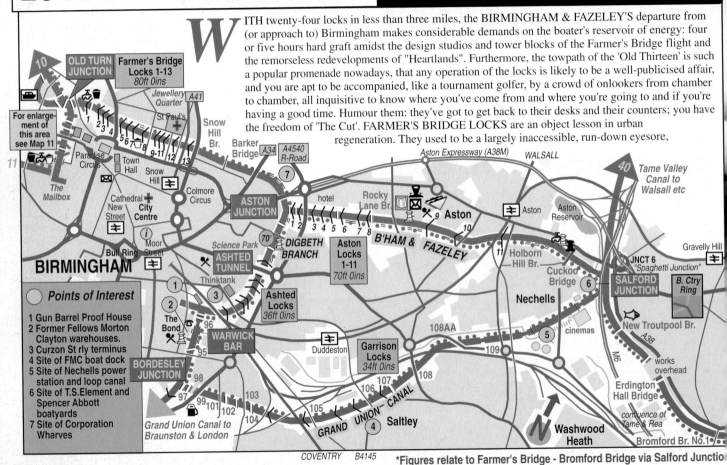

Points of Interest

1 Gun Barrel Proof House
2 Former Fellows Morton Clayton warehouses.
3 Curzon St rly terminus
4 Site of FMC boat dock
5 Site of Nechells power station and loop canal
6 Site of T.S.Element and Spencer Abbott boatyards
7 Site of Corporation Wharves

*Figures relate to Farmer's Bridge - Bromford Bridge via Salford Junction

a boil on Birmingham's bottom, suffering from years of neglect following the demise of commercial carrying in the early Sixties. In 1984 a programme of renewal got under way sponsored by the Birmingham Inner City Partnership. Using Gas Street to Aston as a prototype, BICP set about resurfacing the towpath, improving and increasing access, landscaping, lighting and general restoration at a cost of a cool million. The scheme's impact was considerable. It introduced Brummies to a well-kept secret aspect of their city, and they came to discover it in droves, so that now it hooches with shop and office staff on warm weekday lunchtimes and family groups on postprandial Sunday walks. Joggers relish it too, extending their limbs and expending their energy up and down the ribbed brick surfaces of the refurbished towpath in a distant echo of the hurrying boatmen of the past.

Farmer's Bridge Locks

Farmer's Bridge Locks pass dramatically beneath the commercial core of the city. Each time we visit here more change has accrued - redeveloping the redeveloped one might put it. Locks 10 and 11 lie in a cavern beneath British Telecom's communications tower. There's access here over an easily vaulted wall on to Ludgate Hill and the calm oasis of St Paul's Square, nicknamed the 'Jeweller's Church' because of its connections with the adjoining Jewellery Quarter, a fascinating corner of old Birmingham. Between Locks 12 and 13 the canal negotiates a huge vault under Snow Hill railway station; closed and subsequently demolished at some cost in 1972, but re-opened and rebuilt at more cost (though less style) just fifteen years later.

Lock 13 marks the foot of the flight and is overlooked by a Salvation Army hostel. Two streets away from the mobile-phone-wielding go-getters of Ludgate Hill are the derelicts of Old Snow Hill - the Good Lord giveth and the Good Lord taketh away. Between Snow Hill and Aston the canal, clear of locks for a brief respite, widens and is less claustrophobically engulfed by the high canyons of industry and commerce. The most significant feature of this section - apart from the switchback side bridges which formerly gave access to the Corporation wharves - is the handsome BARKER BRIDGE, a graceful span of cast iron supported by brick piers and abutments dating from 1842.

Aston Locks

A Horseley Iron Works cast iron roving bridge marks the junction of the Birmingham & Fazeley Canal with the Digbeth Branch at Aston. Its elegance, amounting almost to a misleading fragility, is in marked contrast to the overpowering concrete edifice of the adjacent Expressway. Time and time again exploration of the BCN emphasises the great gulf in aesthetic achievement between the civil engineering of the last century and this. Time alters perception, but it does seem inconceivable that any age will ever be able to indentify beauty in the Aston Expressway - but then again!

The canalscape of ASTON LOCKS has benefitted - and we use the term relatively - from the redevelopment zone of *Heartlands*, yet there remains a real sense of isolation, more pronounced the further down the flight you go.

Access to and from the canal has been provided at Holborn Hill Bridge. Easy, then, to use Aston railway station as a staging post: a five minute train ride out from New Street followed by a healthy hour's walk back along the towpath to the city centre. Nearby, one of the earliest main line railways crosses the canal by Lock 11. Opened in 1839, only fifty years after the canal, it linked Birmingham with the North-west. Moorings and a water point are provided by CUCKOO BRIDGE.

Salford Junction

Only a fraction of the stressed-out motorists, fighting their way around the confusion of Gravelley Hill Interchange (aka Spaghetti Junction) are aware of the older, less frenzied meeting and parting of ways engulfed in the concrete gloom below. But such is SALFORD JUNCTION, where the Grand Union Canal's 'Saltley Cut' and Tame Valley Canal - both dating from 1844 - form a canal crossroads with the Birmingham & Fazeley Canal. It's a sobering spot for contemplating Man's contribution to the landscape. Monstrously compromised, the River Tame churns despondently through artificial channels beneath successive generations of civil engineering. Tier upon tier of roadway spirals above you. Little groups of earnest middle management, self-conscious in safety helmets, huddle over calculators, extrapolating infinity.

Whilst ASTON LOCKS represent the most obvious, time efficient

route for boaters tackling the "Black Country Ring", a fascinating alternative for diehards (or indeed as part of a self-contained circular itinerary on foot or afloat) can be made up out of the Digbeth Branch and Grand Union Canal via Bordesley and Saltley as described below.

The Digbeth Branch

Opened in 1799, the Digbeth Branch descends through half a dozen locks from Aston Junction to Warwick Bar, terminating now in a pair of foreshortened basins once lucratively busy with trade to and from Digbeth's many food factories like Typhoo Tea and HP Sauce. It's a secretive section of urban canal of unique character and appeal. All but the top lock have extended side pounds, whilst the chambers have single gates top and bottom as per BCN practice. 48 hour visitor moorings are to be found in the relative secutity and calm of Aston Science Park with a handy winding hole nearby.

Below the bottom lock the original sandstone arch of the Grand Junction Railway's line into Curzon Street station provides a portal into a curvaceous, sepulchral 'tunnel' of railway lines, beyond which the canal opens out to Digbeth (or Proof House) Junction. The alternative name - also used by the adjoining maze of railway tracks - reflects the proximity of the Gun Barrel Proof House of 1813, a strikingly handsome building, with a Jacobean air, overlooking a cobbled courtyard. Above the entrance door is a colourful, three-dimensional military sculpture and the inscription: "Established by Act of Parliament for Public Security." Another nearby building of immense significance is the old Curzon Street station, terminus of the London & Birmingham Railway, whilst the new Thinktank science museum is also readily accesible.

Warwick Bar & Bordesley Junction

Whereas the 'Worcester Bar' at Gas Street lies on a well-trodden tourist trail, the 'Warwick Bar' in Digbeth lies off the beaten track in a 'backstreet' Birmingham still replete with cast iron urinals and pubs offering beer at £1.50 a pint. Here a stop lock was constructed to separate the valuable waters of the Birmingham & Fazeley (later BCN) and Warwick & Birmingham canal companies, and it has recently been cosmetically reinstated to illustrate the deadly rivalry which existed between the two

companies. But whilst the environs and towpath have been much refurbished, the location still has an 'out on a limb' feel, resonantly retaining the ambience of its working past. Alongside the remains of the stop lock stands a warehouse with an awning supported by cast-iron pillars over an arm lying parallel to the narrows. At one time it was leased by Geest the fruit importers and earned the sobriquet 'Banana Warehouse'. Earlier still it belonged to Pickfords, canal carriers of some importance before they made their name with heavy road transport. Nearby is New Warwick Wharf, marked by the tall curved wall of Fellows, Morton & Clayton's warehouse built in 1935 following modernisation of the canal from London. This confident 'Art Deco' style of architecture - emblazoned with the company's name along Fazeley Street to this day - was not rewarded by a significant increase in trade, and, having been for a number of years used by HP Sauces, it now houses a conglomeration of small businesses. Likewise FMC's adjoining Fazeley Street depot, separated from the newer building by an aqueduct over the turgid waters of the River Rea. Built of alternate courses of red and blue brick, and equipped with weatherboarded elevators and an attractive saw-tooth valanced canopy over a side arm, this older grouping of warehouses has been redeveloped as 'The Bond', a centre for graphic art based businesses featuring a pleasant cafe - limited moorings are available here in a secure setting - Tel: 0121-766 7400. Directly opposite the towpath rises and falls over a side bridge spanning an arm which once led into one of the City of Birmingham's Salvage Department basins. Horsedrawn rubbish boats operated between here and the Small Heath destructor until 1965. The high arch of a ruined railway viaduct frames the canal near Bridge 95.

The Saltley Cut

Surrounded by gloomy factory walls, BORDESLEY JUNCTION is spanned by a graceful roving bridge cast by Lloyds & Fosters. Immediately southwards the Grand Union Canal commences the climb to its Olton Summit via Camp Hill Locks, a route covered in our *South Midlands Canal Companion*. Likewise the Saltley Cut, barely industrial now as neat blocks of new housing overlook a towpath burgeoning with poppies, cranesbill, dog rose and daisies: a fecundity derived from generations of boat horse dung perhaps.

MINWORTH used to mark the frontier between open country and the West Midlands conurbation, but the building of a high tech business park on the towpath side between Minworth Green and Wigginshill Road bridges has blurred the once distinct boundary. Corn fields remain defiantly agricultural on the opposite bank, but the more cynical may feel that it is only a matter of time before the prices for building land outweigh the marginal profits of the annual harvest. Furthermore, the new orbital toll road is planned to cross the canal somewhere around here, so enjoy the serenity while you can.

If, then, you want to avoid overnight mooring in a built-up area, you would be advised to tie up no further west than "The Kingsley" steak bar by Wigginshill Road Bridge. Not that the stretch of canal between Bromford and Minworth is uninteresting. Reference to three twentieth century maps revealed a steady cycle of change. In 1916 the tyre makers Dunlop built a huge works on a 400 acre greenfield site which became known as Fort Dunlop. To transport the workforce to and from this new plant, the company operated a small fleet of passenger carrying narrowboats between Aston and Bromford until the neighbouring Tyburn Road was laid with tram tracks. Apparently the two and a half mile, lock-free journey took around half an hour and each boat could seat a hundred passengers.

In 1938 the fields east of Fort Dunlop were occupied by one of the 'shadow' munitions factories as Britain armed for war. During the next seven years over eleven thousand Spitfires were built at the plant. The works was handily placed for test flights, for across the Chester Road stood Castle Bromwich Aerodrome which had hosted Birmingham's very first flying demonstration in 1911. After the Second World War the aerodrome was run down and replaced, in the early Sixties, by the sprawling estate of Castle Vale: five thousand homes in blocks of flats rising to sixteen floors. Social problems? What social problems?

In his book *No.1*, former canal boat captain, Tom Foxon, wrote in detail of his experiences on the Birmingham & Fazeley in the mid 1950s. At that time substantial tonnages of coal were still being carried by canal from the collieries of North Warwickshire to the factory furnaces of Birmingham aboard 'Joey boats', boatman's parlance for narrowboats used for short-haul work and not designed for living aboard. The men who worked these largely horse-drawn boats knew this canal as the 'Old Cut' and in his book Tom describes the working practices of the era, commenting wryly that this was the most depressing route experienced in his boating career. You'll just have to take it from us that matters have improved since those days - well relatively! Near Minworth Green, a roving bridge marks the site of a dock used to unload ash for use in the filter beds of the adjoining sewage plant.

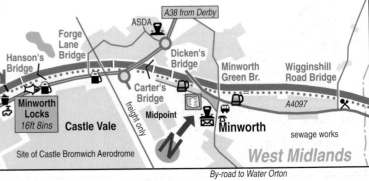

WHO loves the Birmingham & Fazeley? It's not the most charismatic of canals, though it certainly provides a useful link between the canals of the east and west midlands, and is a constituent of the popular Black Country and Warwickshire 'rings'. Here, spending five miles or so in the company of the county of Warwickshire, it traverses a largely agricultural landscape interspersed with gravel pits. The M42 motorway runs parallel to the canal and the new Birmingham Northern Relief Toll road crosses it, its construction necessitating repositioning of the Top Lock and the demolition of the lock-keeper's house at Dunton Wharf. The canal cottages along this length are numbered in the BCN sequence, a reminder that the B&F merged with the

Birmingham Canal Navigations in 1794. Not far north from Dunton Wharf, along the A446 is the Belfry Hotel and its famous golf course. Another sporting association belongs to Bodymoor Heath where Aston Villa, the Birmingham football club, have their training ground. Canalside at Cheatle's Farm Bridge stands the "Dog & Doublet", an unspoilt Georgian pub with attractive wood interiors. It attracts a strong local following of motorised visitors as well as canal travellers.

The bottom lock of the Curdworth flight is overlooked by a quartet of canal cottages. Life must be pleasant here if, as one supposes, the inhabitants find the isolation conducive. Skeins of geese rise into the wide skies from flooded gravel workings. But for the distant clatter of machinery it could be some remote East Anglian marsh. Gravel has been extracted from the valley of the Tame since the 1930s. Originally by dredger, later by dragline. Nowadays conveyor belts carry the minerals to screening and washing plants where they are sorted into varying types of aggregates. The landscape might have been irrevocably scarred by such activities were it not for the imaginative creation of KINGSBURY WATER PARK out of the abandoned gravel workings. Moorings are available above the bottom lock and it's but a short walk to the park's Visitor Centre (Tel: 01827 872660).

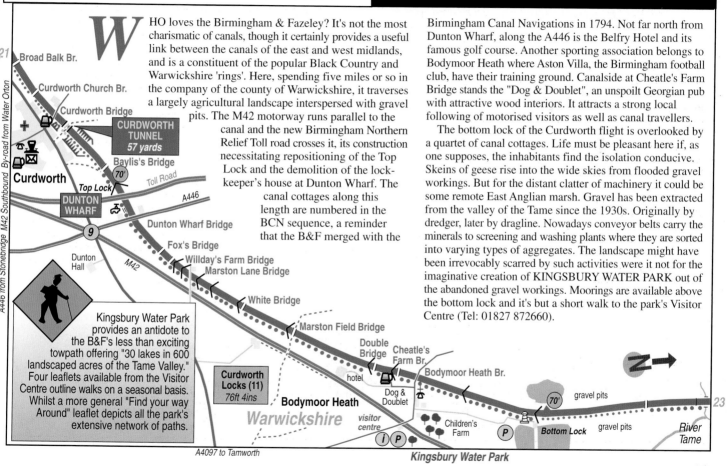

Kingsbury Water Park provides an antidote to the B&F's less than exciting towpath offering "30 lakes in 600 landscaped acres of the Tame Valley." Four leaflets available from the Visitor Centre outline walks on a seasonal basis. Whilst a more general "Find your way Around" leaflet depicts all the park's extensive network of paths.

FAZELEY JUNCTION isn't anywhere near as pretty as Fradley, but it exudes a certain grubby grandeur, exemplified by the handsome junction house and the big mills which might have escaped from Oldham or Rochdale. The Birmingham & Fazeley reached here in 1789 and the following year Sir Robert Peel (father of the Prime Minister) opened a mill for cotton spinning and calico printing. It was powered by the waters of the Bourne Brook which joins the Tame nearby. A second mill, of five towering storeys, was erected in 1883 for the weaving of haberdashery and upholstery. Both mills remain more or less intact for the entertainment of the industrial archaeologist. East of Fazeley Junction the Coventry Canal heads off for Nuneaton, Hawkesbury and Braunston as covered by our *South Midlands Canal Companion*. South of Fazeley lies one of the 'little wonders' of the inland waterways, the exotic Drayton footbridge, where two Gothic towers

encase spiral staircases and support an otherwise pretty ordinary open iron span; a delightful functional folly: have your camera ready.

British Waterways regional offices overlook the canal at PEEL'S WHARF, along with adjoining housing, the sale of which presumably paid for the offices. More new housing has materialised on the opposite bank, whilst a new dual-carriageway section of the A5 has effectively vanquished the former peace and quiet of the broadwater by Bonehill Bridge. There are glimpses to the north of Tamworth Castle and the imposing parish church of St Editha, before the canal escapes the clutches of the retail parks and loses itself in and amongst the cabbage fields - which it is often called upon to irrigate - before reaching Hopwas.

Middleton Hall

A4091 from Birmingham

By-roads from Drayton Bassett

A5 Northbound

A453 from Sutton Coldfield

Balls Bridge

22

Fisher's Mill Br.

Drayton Brick Br.

Drayton Footbridge & Swivelbridge

Drayton Manor Park

B.C.R.

Debbies Dayboats

70'

Tolson's Foot-bridge

PEEL'S WHARF

mills

Dunstall Farm Br.

Dunstall Br.

Bonehill Bridge

Retail Park

Sutton Road Br.

River Tame

BW Regional Office

Coleshill Road Br.

River Tame

Mill Marina

FAZELEY JUNCTION

Staffordshire

Fazeley

Coventry Canal to Tamworth   A5 Southbound   Tamworth Town Centre

NOT generally thought of as a beautiful canal, the Coventry nevertheless becomes almost picturesque in its wandering between Fazeley and Huddlesford; particularly as it ghosts through the brackeny woodlands of Hopwas, where red flags warn of military manoeuvres. Glibly we call this the Coventry Canal, but actually - and by now the presence of nameplates and not numbers on the bridges should have quickened your suspicions - the canal between Fazeley and Whittington was built by the Birmingham & Fazeley company. The Coventry Canal received its Act of Parliament in 1768, but seventeen years later it was nowhere near completion; primarily through a shortage of capital, but also, historians suspect, because some of the directors had interests in the Warwickshire coalfield and were worried by the thought that their through route, were it to be finished, would boost trade from the North Staffordshire pits at the expense of their own. In frustration the Trent & Mersey and Birmingham & Fazeley companies undertook to jointly build the canal between Fazeley and Fradley. The two met at Whittington in 1790, at a point graced with a plaque provided by the local branch of the I.W.A. commemorating the bicentenary of the joining.

So pleasant scenery and canal history mingle as you negotiate the lower valley of the Tame; passing Fisherwick, where the houses face the canal in Dutch fashion, rather than turning their backs on it as is more often the case in England; and arcing round Whittington, where one of the canalside gardens is graced with its own decorative lock. Huddlesford 'Junction' has been something of a misnomer since the Wyrley & Essington Canal was closed between here and Ogley (near Brownhills) in the Fifties;

the Lichfield and Hatherton Canals Restoration Trust, figure-headed by the actor David Suchet (best known as Hercule Poirot in the Agatha Christie television adaptions) are determined that these two 'back door' entries to the Birmingham Canal Navigations will be restored to full navigation. These are enlightened times as far as canal restorationists are concerned, and as the 'second generation' of re-opened canals come on stream, enthusiasts are looking ahead to a new era of canal refurbishment on routes never thought likely to be navigable again.

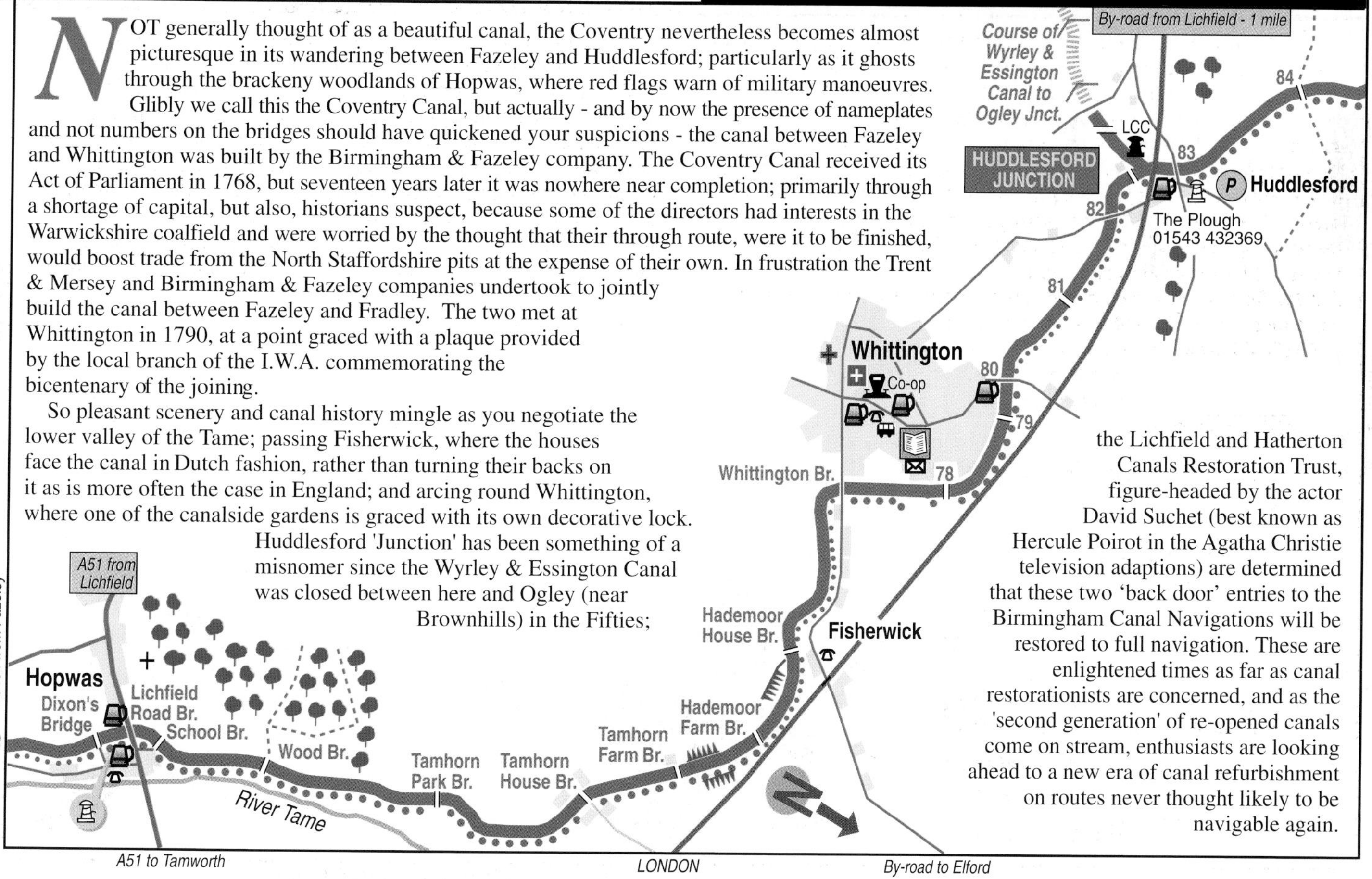

Course of Wyrley & Essington Canal to Ogley Jnct.

By-road from Lichfield - 1 mile

84

25

LCC

83

82

HUDDLESFORD JUNCTION

P Huddlesford

The Plough
01543 432369

81

Whittington

Co-op

80

79

Whittington Br.

78

Hademoor House Br.

Fisherwick

A51 from Lichfield

Hopwas

Dixon's Bridge

Lichfield Road Br. School Br.

Wood Br.

Tamhorn Park Br.

Tamhorn House Br.

Tamhorn Farm Br.

Hademoor Farm Br.

River Tame

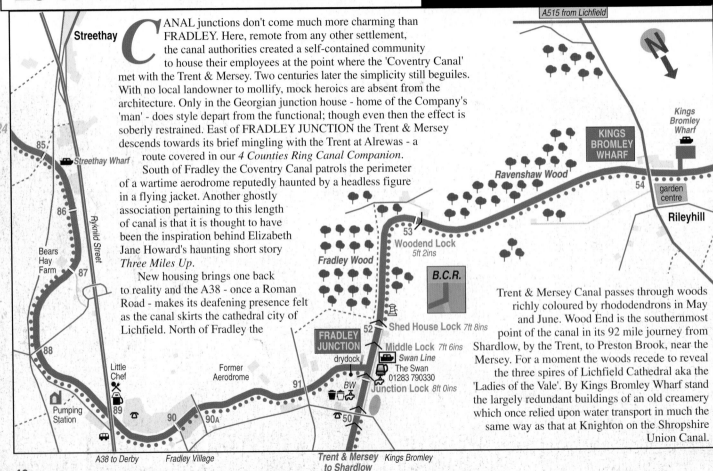

Streethay

CANAL junctions don't come much more charming than FRADLEY. Here, remote from any other settlement, the canal authorities created a self-contained community to house their employees at the point where the 'Coventry Canal' met with the Trent & Mersey. Two centuries later the simplicity still beguiles. With no local landowner to mollify, mock heroics are absent from the architecture. Only in the Georgian junction house - home of the Company's 'man' - does style depart from the functional; though even then the effect is soberly restrained. East of FRADLEY JUNCTION the Trent & Mersey descends towards its brief mingling with the Trent at Alrewas - a route covered in our *4 Counties Ring Canal Companion*.

South of Fradley the Coventry Canal patrols the perimeter of a wartime aerodrome reputedly haunted by a headless figure in a flying jacket. Another ghostly association pertaining to this length of canal is that it is thought to have been the inspiration behind Elizabeth Jane Howard's haunting short story *Three Miles Up*.

New housing brings one back to reality and the A38 - once a Roman Road - makes its deafening presence felt as the canal skirts the cathedral city of Lichfield. North of Fradley the

Trent & Mersey Canal passes through woods richly coloured by rhododendrons in May and June. Wood End is the southernmost point of the canal in its 92 mile journey from Shardlow, by the Trent, to Preston Brook, near the Mersey. For a moment the woods recede to reveal the three spires of Lichfield Cathedral aka the 'Ladies of the Vale'. By Kings Bromley Wharf stand the largely redundant buildings of an old creamery which once relied upon water transport in much the same way as that at Knighton on the Shropshire Union Canal.

Map labels:
- A515 from Lichfield
- N
- Kings Bromley Wharf
- KINGS BROMLEY WHARF
- Ravenshaw Wood
- garden centre
- 54
- Rileyhill
- 53
- Woodend Lock 5ft 2ins
- Fradley Wood
- B.C.R.
- Shed House Lock 7ft 8ins
- 52
- Middle Lock 7ft 6ins
- FRADLEY JUNCTION
- drydock
- Swan Line
- The Swan 01283 790330
- BW
- Junction Lock 8ft 0ins
- 50
- Trent & Mersey to Shardlow
- Kings Bromley
- 91
- 90A
- 90
- Former Aerodrome
- Little Chef
- 89
- Pumping Station
- A38 to Derby
- Fradley Village
- 88
- Bears Hay Farm
- 87
- 86
- Ryknild Street
- Bears Hay Farm
- 85
- Streethay Wharf
- 24

Shed House (aka Shadehouse) Lock, Fradley, Trent & Mersey Canal.

BETWEEN Fradley and Handsacre the canal winds through a village-less tract of country, comprehensively agricultural now, but betraying signs of the wild heathland it must once have been in its sandy soil, gorse, bracken and gnarled oaks.

Armitage and Shanks are synonymous with toilet plumbing, their trade marks are emblazoned on public conveniences throughout the world. Once they were separate firms - they merged in 1969 - but the site alongside the canal at ARMITAGE dates back to 1817. Sanitaryware became a speciality in the 19th century under the management of Edward Johns - the origin of the Americanism 'going to the John'. Today the factory is huge and convincingly prosperous, and Armitage Shanks are a public limited company with a seemingly 'watertight' future.

Connections are apparent with another famous earthenware firm at Spode House and Hawkesyard Priory. Josiah Spode, a member of the North Staffordshire pottery family, left his house to a Dominican Order in 1893 and the monks proceeded to build a priory in the grounds. The priory is now a nursing home whilst the house and its grounds have been converted into a golf course.

Passing beneath the A513, the canal narrows and negotiates a rocky cutting. One-way working is the order of the day. This was formerly the site of Armitage (or "Plum Pudding") Tunnel, a dramatic, unlined bore through the rock face. Subsidence, brought about by coal mining, necessitated opening out of the tunnel, and concrete lining of the canal banks. Not that mining is any longer an activity associated with the area. Lea Hall Colliery, which stood canalside by Bridge 63 since opening in 1960, had been a modern showcase pit for the NCB, much of its output making the shortest of journeys to the adjacent power station. But it closed in 1990 and was rapidly demolished, an industrial estate being developed on its site.

From Bridge 58 it's but a short stroll to the old High Bridge across the Trent. It's been by-passed by progress and unsightly girders support its once graceful cast iron span, but its interest lies in the fact that it was made at Coalbrookdale in 1830.

Towpath improvements are taking place, for this stretch of canal is now part of Staffordshire's "Millennium Way", a route for walkers, horse-riders and cyclists between Newport and Burton-on-Trent.

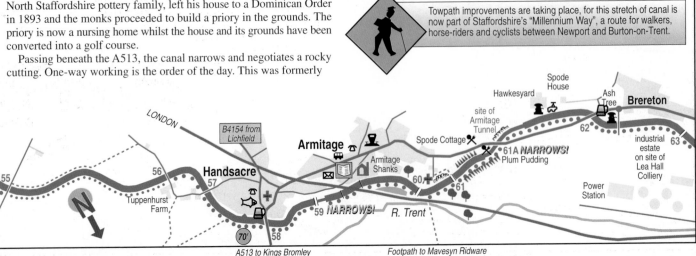

THE river's slow influence pervades the canal, and the pair wander across the landscape like indolent lovers on a long afternoon, chaperoned at a discreet distance by the recumbent mass of The Chase. Several big houses were built by prosperous landowners in this enchanting countryside. The stuccoed facade of Bishton Hall overlooks the canal. Nowadays it is a prep school with a cricket ground shaded by ancient chestnut trees bordering the water. Another mansion, Wolseley Hall, stood opposite on the far bank of the river. It was demolished long ago, but the grounds have become home to a garden centre. Wolseley Bridge has graced the Trent here since 1800. It was designed by John Rennie, best known in canal circles for his work on the Kennet & Avon. The "Staffordshire Way" joins the towpath at Bridge 68 and follows the canal as far as Great Haywood, before disappearing off into the grounds of Shugborough on its way to the southernmost tip of the county at Kinver Edge.

RUGELEY gets a bad press from most guide-books which condescend to mention it at all, but we like the sheer up-front ugliness of the place, and its refusal to pretend to be what it patently isn't; pretty! Once it had two dubious claims to fame: its malodorous tannery and its connections with the notorious Victorian poisoner, William Palmer. But the tannery and the poisoner no longer impinge, and it is the power station which dominates now, having been opened here in the Sixties to take advantage of coal mined on the spot. At Brindley Bank the canal suddenly stops running parallel to the Trent and turns sharply to cross it, as though Brindley had been screwing up his courage to bridge the river. A handsome pumping station overlooks this crossing of water over water, though the aqueduct itself is nothing to write home about.

By Bridge 68 a short reedy arm adjacent to the railway provides a useful turning point for lengthy craft. It occurs to us that this may have been used as a transhipment basin in the fledgling days of the railway, perhaps for the conveyance of building materials.

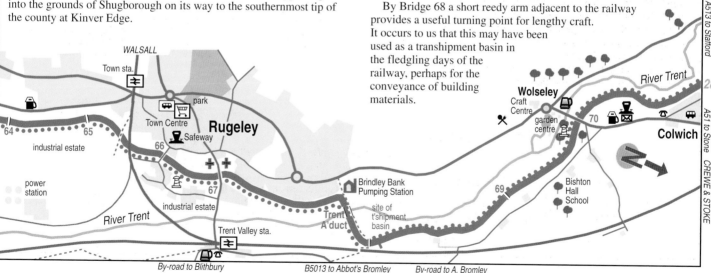

BRINDLEY always found it easier to follow river valleys, and Great Haywood was an obvious choice of location for a canal junction designed to establish his scheme for a 'Grand Cross' of man made waterways linking the four great English estuaries: Humber, Thames, Severn and Mersey. With the completion of the Staffordshire & Worcestershire Canal in 1772, and the Trent & Mersey five years later, Haywood became a canal junction of major importance, as significant to transport in the 18th century as any motorway interchange today. One is only left to marvel at the simplicity of it all - two quiet ribbons of water meeting beneath a bridge of exquisite beauty - and compare it sadly with transport interchanges of the 20th century, acres of concrete, noise and pollution. Where did we go wrong? History may have taken some wrong turnings, but there is little chance for the canal traveller to make a mistake, for a prominent fingerpost directs one concisely enough to "Wolverhampton", "The Trent", or "The Potteries". Between here and Colwich the TRENT & MERSEY is at its most memorably beautiful as it skirts the boundary of Shugborough. On one bank beechwoods tumble

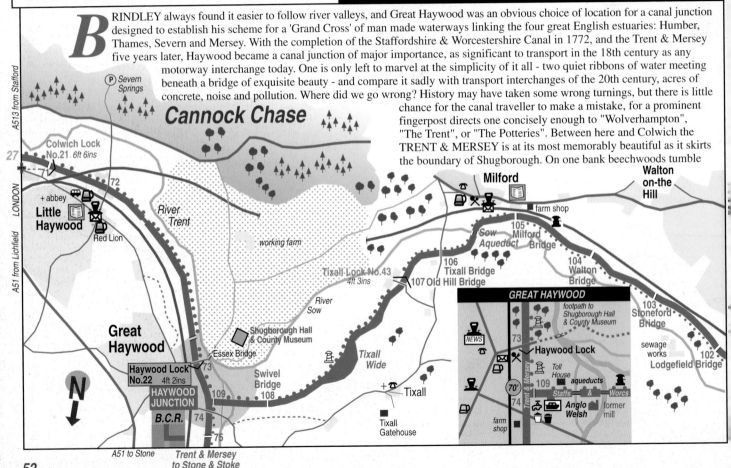

down to the water's edge. On the other, across the Trent, there are glimpses of the curious statues, antiquities and follies which pepper the grounds of this famous home of the Anson family. Colwich Lock lies in an attractive setting between the village church, a picturesque farm, and a bend in the river. From Bridge 72 you can take an idyllic walk to Severn Springs, a wonderful springboard for exploring Cannock Chase.

The Staffordshire & Worcestershire Canal

Through the arch of Bridge 109 - an 18th century fusion of functional engineering and enduring loveliness - the Staffordshire & Worcestershire Canal commences its 46 mile journey down to the Severn at Stourport. Two aqueducts carry it across the Trent and a millstream. A couple of miles further on it crosses the Sow. Between these river crossings the canal suddenly casts off its inhibitions and widens into a broad lake of quite un-canal-like proportions, bordered by thick reedbeds inhabited by a gorgeous array of wildfowl. Boaters will find their craft looping the loop out of sheer exuberance. This is Tixall Wide or Broadwater and there are two theories for its surprising existence. Some maintain that the canal was widened into an artificial lake to placate the owner of Tixall Hall. Others that the expanse of water predates the canal, that it was naturally formed, and that Izaak Walton learnt to fish here. Whichever explanation suits you, don't miss the extraordinary Elizabethan gatehouse which overlooks the Wide. The hall itself, where Mary Queen of Scots was imprisoned for a fortnight in 1586, was demolished long ago. The gatehouse is let for holidays by the Landmark Trust - Tel: 01628 825925.

West of Tixall's solitary lock the canal meanders enchantingly through the valley of the Sow. A plethora of trees adds lustre to the landscape. The river is crossed by way of a typical low-slung Brindley masonry aqueduct. Bridge 105 is a handsome turnover affair from which there is access under the railway to the village of Milford. Between here and Baswich the canal runs through fields between the river and the railway whose southbound trains are quickly gobbled up by the decorated portal of Shugborough Tunnel.

Great Haywood

Keith Goss

LARGELY unmolested, the canal slips quietly through the outskirts of Stafford. The county town stood an aloof mile to the west of the Staffs & Worcs Canal which, in true Brindley fashion, followed the easy contours of the Penk Valley. Plans to construct a branch were dropped in favour of a simple lock down into the Sow, the river being dredged and realigned to take boats as far as a terminal basin at Green Bridge in the centre of Stafford. The navigation was opened in 1816 and in use until the end of the First World War. A footpath follows the riverbank into the town, but it's difficult to imagine how seventy foot narrowboats ever got up there!

Baswich church once stood as isolated on its hillside as Acton Trussell's does still, but now it is surrounded by a housing development, though those with an interest in ecclesiastical architecture can easily reach it from Bridge 100. Note the spelling of the village's name with a 'k' on the bridgeplate. There was a substantial wharf by Radford Bridge, but its site is now somewhat less interestingly occupied by a car showroom following demolition of the original warehouses in the Philistine Seventies.

Stafford Boat Club - with their impressive club house - occupy a former brickworks arm near Hazelstrine Bridge. Most of the works's output was despatched by canal. Bridge 97 has disappeared completely, there being not even any tell-tale narrowing in the canal's channel where it once must have stood. Hereabouts the inherent other-worldliness of the waterway undergoes strange, paradoxical fluctuations in fortune. Nowhere could be more apparently remote than Deptmore Lock, where the reclusive inhabitant of the rose-clad cottages commutes to the outside world by dinghy. Elsewhere, however, the M6 threatens to intrude like an unwelcome caller on your afternoon off; whilst Acton Trussell, which you'd expect with such a name to be a picture book English village, disappoints with its banal modern architecture. Similarly Wildwood, which ought to be the home of friendly, furry little creatures straight out of some children's tale, has become a housing estate on a hill. But when vapours rise off the Penk, and its marshy meadows ooze sponge-like with excess water, a return to an older, more elemental existence seems somehow tangible, and man's scars upon the landscape recede into the mists of time.

Acton's houses attract a following of ducks. The solitary building on the towpath side used to be a boatman's pub. Present day boaters, however, slake their thirst in the old moated house by Bridge 92, opened a few years ago as a bar and restaurant set in charming grounds. It is said that Brindley actually used the old house's moat for a few yards when building the canal.

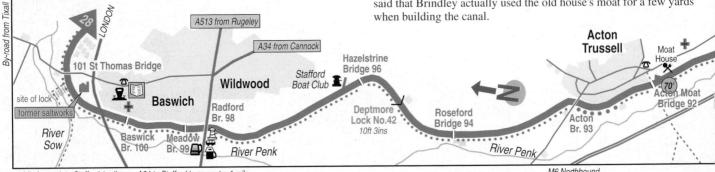

A S the canal ascends to (or descends from) its summit level, the locks come thick and fast. The motorway retreats, only to be replaced by the housing estates which cling-wrap the otherwise agreeable little town of Penkridge. Yet, a mile on either side, the countryside is characterised by rolling farmland lifting to the bulwark of Cannock Chase.

The towpath between bridges 90 and 86 is hi-jacked by the "Staffordshire Way" which seems forever to be bumping into canals and appropriating towpaths in the course of its 92 mile journey from Mow Cop to Kinver Edge. Its route has come down off The Chase and crossed Teddesley Park. Teddesley Hall was the seat of Sir Edward Littleton, one of the chief promoters of the Staffordshire & Worcestershire Canal. Indeed, the family remained involved with the canal company until its nationalisation in 1947. The hall itself was demolished by the army (!) in the mid Fifties (having been used as a prison camp for German officers during the Second World War) but the estate farm remains, hidden from the canal by some woodland known as Wellington Belt in commemoration of a visit to the hall by the Iron Duke. Bridge 89 once had ornate balustrades commensurate with its importance as the gateway to the hall, but sadly these have been infilled by brickwork.

PENKRIDGE WHARF is quieter than of late, no longer being the location of a busy boat hire base. Boats still pause here to take on water, however, and there is usually room to moor up for a visit to the town. The Littletons had fingers in many pies, not least the local colliery, which at one time employed over a thousand men. A huge basin, now covered by the motorway, was constructed to enable boats to be loaded with coal from a raised pier by gravity. The chief traffic flow of Littleton coal by canal in later years was down to Stourport power station as noted on Map 1.

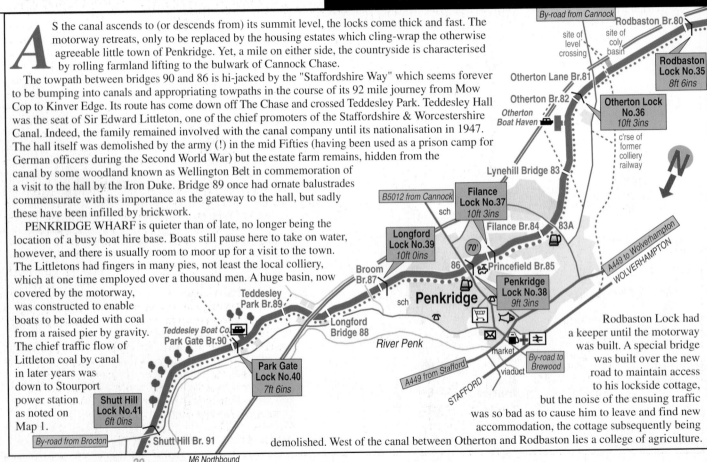

Rodbaston Lock had a keeper until the motorway was built. A special bridge was built over the new road to maintain access to his lockside cottage, but the noise of the ensuing traffic was so bad as to cause him to leave and find new accommodation, the cottage subsequently being demolished. West of the canal between Otherton and Rodbaston lies a college of agriculture.

CALF HEATH is a strangely isolated tract of country, pancake flat and crossed by a grid of sullen little roads, with here and there a huddle of houses, gathered reassuringly together like something out of Van Gogh's early potato field paintings. The canal all but boxes the compass of this gravel pit-riddled landscape, so that the Chase with its communications tower and the chemical works with its phalanx of flaring chimneys, appear to move about you, teasing you into geographic insecurity, like a game of Blind Man's Buff.

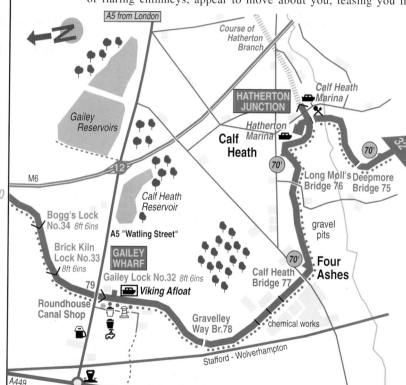

The Staffs & Worcs Canal's summit - from Gailey to Compton (Map 6) - lies at more or less 340 feet above sea level. If you've climbed up from Penkridge and beyond it's a relief to be done with locks for the time being, though for those on an anti-clockwise "Black Country Ring" itinerary the prospect of the Wolverhampton 'Twenty-One' can be quite daunting. Industry lines the canal at Four Ashes. The old tar works here was once served by Thomas Clayton boats.

The last load of Cannock coal came off the Hatherton Branch in 1949 and it was abandoned a couple of years later. However, the illusion of a junction remains, because the bottom lock (of what was once a flight of eight in three miles) is still used to provide access to moorings. The Lichfield and Hatherton Canals Restoration Trust is actively seeking restoration of the branch with the intention of linking it with the northern waters of the BCN at Norton Canes.

Watling Street crosses the canal at Gailey. The most significant feature here is the 'round house', originally a toll clerk's office but now a splendid canal shop. There is something spellbinding about cylindrical buildings - Martello towers, windmills, lighthouses; even Birmingham's Bull Ring Rotunda - and Gailey round house, in its lock-side setting, has a particular charm which you will want to try and capture on film.

The Roundhouse is run by mother and daughter team, Eileen and Karen Lester. Eileen has been involved with canals for many years and also works for Water Travel at Aldersley Junction. Karen is something of a wordsmith, having published her own volume of canal inspired verse called *Off the Straight & Narrow*.

THE canal exchanges the loneliness of Calf and Coven heaths for the industrial and suburban outskirts of Wolverhampton; the M54 to Telford forming an obvious, though not intentional, boundary. At Cross Green a former boatman's pub called "The Anchor" has become the "Fox & Anchor", a popular restaurant bar, and many boaters choose to moor here overnight. As it passes beneath the M54 the canal crosses the county boundary between Staffordshire and the West Midlands, one of the new counties which had its origins in the local government changes of 1974. Many people still mourn the old counties. It must have been galling, for instance, to have lived in Lincolnshire all one's life and wake up one morning in South Humberside. West Midlands was possibly the dullest of all the new names, and sounds as though it must have been the compromise of a committee. Black Country would have been a far more appropriate and resonant title. You can imagine its inhabitants

espousing a perverse pride in such a name, no-one could possibly show a flicker of interest in anyone who admitted to coming from the West Midlands! The most significant feature of this length is "Pendeford Rockin", the old boatmen's name for a shallow, but tellingly narrow cutting hewn by Brindley's navvies through a solid belt of sandstone which breaks through the clay strata at this point. The cutting, half a mile or so long, restricts the channel to such a degree that you begin to wonder if you have lost concentration and taken a wrong turn. There are, however, one or two passing places - as on a single lane road - where oncoming boats can be successfully negotiated without losing one's temper. Similar narrows occur on the Shropshire Union north of Autherley as that canal encounters the same difficult rock.

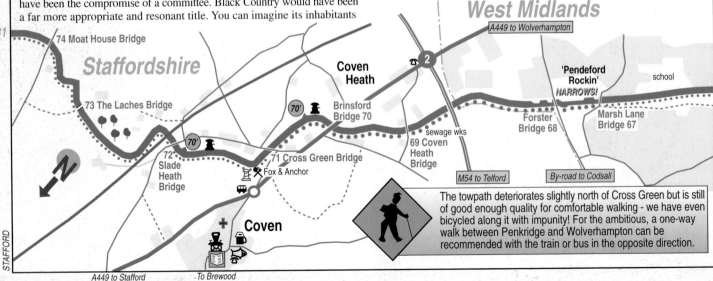

The towpath deteriorates slightly north of Cross Green but is still of good enough quality for comfortable walking - we have even bicycled along it with impunity! For the ambitious, a one-way walk between Penkridge and Wolverhampton can be recommended with the train or bus in the opposite direction.

Locking up the Stourbridge 16

THE Canal Companions, it is widely known, have a tendency to wax lyrical. In these pages, at least, the spirit of romance remains alive and - not so much kicking as - soft shoe shuffling. So when we tell you that the pound between Stourton and Wordsley is simply ravishing, the cynics will have to take it with a pinch of salt. Frankly, though, there is a precarious beauty about the Stourbridge Canal as it winds past Primrose Hill and through woodland above the Stour which, is only to be equalled by the Caldon Canal in the Churnet Valley. On one of many cruises over this length, we picnicked by Bell's Mill Bridge on a hot September noon, wandered down to the footbridge over the Stour, saw a kingfisher flash beneath us, and met a lady on the towpath who didn't bat an eyelid when Eden, then aged four, asked if she was aware that "foxes didn't eat people." Memories are made of this. You will have your own from this spellbinding stretch of canal.

A modest, twin-arched aqueduct over the Stour stands close by WORDSLEY JUNCTION and the opportunity for a detour up the branch to the excellent moorings at Stourbridge Town Wharf. The arm terminates at the foot of Stourbridge High Street (though it once proceeded a short distance beyond to a railway transhipment basin) beside a restored bonded warehouse with an upper storey supported by cast iron columns. Secure moorings are provided by the Stourbridge Navigation Trust (Tel: 01384 395216) free of charge (though donations are welcomed for longer stays) and this a thoroughly pleasant spot for an overnight stay, though its increasing popularity may mean that you have to tie up some distance short of the terminal winding hole and its security zone.

The arm itself has much interest and incident packed into its one and three eighth mile length: the old Dial glass works by Chubbs Bridge; Coalbourn Brook Bridge which used to carry the Kinver Light Railway

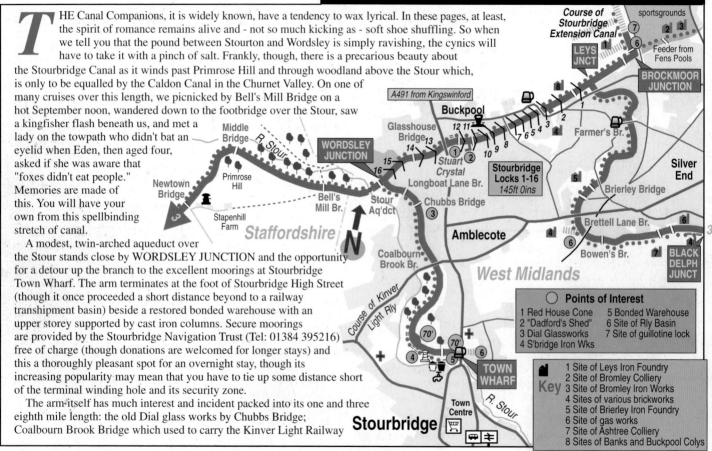

Points of Interest
1 Red House Cone
2 "Dadford's Shed"
3 Dial Glassworks
4 S'bridge Iron Wks
5 Bonded Warehouse
6 Site of Rly Basin
7 Site of guillotine lock

Key
1 Site of Leys Iron Foundry
2 Site of Bromley Colliery
3 Site of Bromley Iron Works
4 Sites of various brickworks
5 Site of Brierley Iron Foundry
6 Site of gas works
7 Site of Ashtree Colliery
8 Sites of Banks and Buckpool Colys

Stourbridge Locks 1-16 145ft 0ins

*Figures refer to main line between Stourton Junction and Black Delph Junction. Allow half an hour in each direction for the Town Arm.

(Map 3); and what remains of Stourbridge Iron Works where the first steam locomotive to operate in the USA was built. Named *Stourbridge Lion*, it puffed its way through Pennsylvania in 1829. The works had been founded by John Bradley in 1798. His name appears on the southernmost roving bridge, a diminutive structure of cast iron construction dated 1873. By this final bend the canal widens, arrowhead flourishes and there is plenty of room to manoeuvre a turn in easier conditions than the crowded end of the arm.

The Stourbridge Sixteen

On a former trip, we came down the Sixteen in a respectable two and a half hours, with a crew of two adults and two children and not another boat in sight. It was two days before Tamar's eleventh birthday and she heroically coped with the flight's stiffish paddle gear. Lockwheeling ahead, it was 'Dad' who had the most problems, with the badly balanced bottom gates of Lock 15, which refused to stay shut simultaneously. It had the makings of a *Candid Camera* spoof as he closed one gate, then ran round via the top of the lock to try and shut the other before the first swung back open. Asking an elderly gentleman for help proved fruitless. "'E's not touching that lock," growled his wife - a belligerent Jack Russell of a woman - "'E's just had an 'art attack!"

The flight is characterised by reedy side ponds aiding and abetting water supply. Furthermore it is accompanied by the spirits of the long deceased industries - coal, clay and iron - whose trade made it so prosperous in its heyday. Most of the evidence of these trades is confined to old maps, but two classic survivors remain in the form of "Dadford's Shed", a former transhipment warehouse built of timber and now partially used by a boatbuilder; and the massive Red House Cone (or kiln) preserved by Stuart Crystal as part of their glass-making visitor centre. Both of these dinosaurs reside in the vicinity of Lock 12, whilst nearby stands "The Dock", a general store and off licence with a tradition of serving boatmen past and present. Locks 9 and 10 are telescoped together like a mini-Bratch, and were similarly once a true staircase. By Lock 4 is the "Samson & Lion", a popular free house, whilst the old "Bottle & Glass", now happily ensconced in the time warp of the Black Country

Living Museum used to stand on the opposite side from the towpath above Lock 3 where the canal widens into what was once a public wharf.

Leys Junction - Black Delph

Leys Junction may not be much to look at now, but it is effectively the custom post to the lost worlds of the Fens Branch and Stourbridge Extension Canal. Navigation is feasible for the committed as far as Brookmoor, but it's the walker who will derive most pleasure from exploring these forgotten routes. Try and get hold of a copy of Ian Langford's *Towpath Guide to the Stourbridge Canal* published by Lapal in 1992 if you want more detail than we have space for here. The main line, however, veers east essaying a serpentine course through housing zones and echoes of industry past and present. Hereabouts - as we remarked in an earlier edition - realisation comes suddenly that you are no longer a holidaymaker, but rather a traveller in the strictest sense of the term, as adventurously off the beaten track as if you were mountain-busting in darkest Peru.

The Stourbridge has a celebrated niche in the story of the post-war canal revival. Trade had largely vanished from this route by the late Fifties and the canal decayed to the point of dereliction. In 1962 the IWA held their National Rally on the Town Arm against the wishes of British Waterways. A series of absurd hostilities ensued which would have furnished the plot of an Ealing comedy. The authorities refused to dredge the canal so the enthusiasts decided to do it themselves. In the November 1987 issue of *Waterways World* restoration luminary, David Hutchings, recalled confronting a BW deputation on the towpath as his dragline was poised to break the choked waters of the arm. Reaching an impasse, both parties repaired to nearby telephone kiosks to seek the advice of their respective solicitors. Hutchings was advised to proceed in 'his usual piratical manner' and, to coin a phrase, British Waterways ended up with mud all over its bureaucratic face. The Stourbridge Rally was a success in its own right and, five years later, after much work had been carried out jointly by BW and volunteers, the Stourbridge Sixteen was re-opened.

At BLACK DELPH JUNCTION the Stourbridge Canal makes an unheralded, end on junction with the Dudley No.1 Canal.

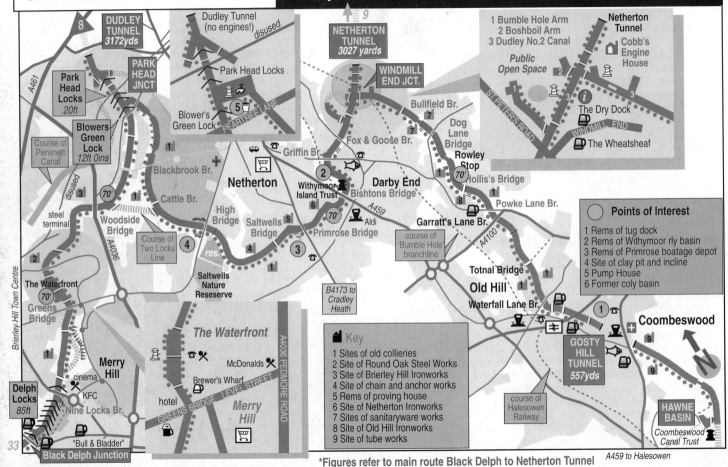

THOUGH amalgamated with the Birmingham Canal Navigations as long ago as 1846, there is about the Dudley Canals an independence of style and spirit which marks them apart from the bulk of the system on the other side of the Rowley Hills. Mid 19th century improvements - by-passing some of the more circuitous loops; construction of Netherton Tunnel; substitution of the original nine locks at The Delph by eight new ones - left their legacy of BCN characteristics. But crossing the 'invisible' junction at the foot of Delph Locks, or emerging from the gloom of Netherton's southern portal, you can almost grasp the change in atmosphere; a new variation on an old theme.

Black Delph - Park Head

THE DELPH was known in the 19th century as 'Black Delph' because of the proliferation of collieries in the vicinity. Nowadays 'Green Delph' would be a more appropriate sobriquet, for barely a vestige of industry remains. Delph Locks consist of eight chambers, of which six are in close proximity, carrying the canal from the 356ft level of the Stourbridge Canal to the 441ft contour of the Dudley No.1 Canal. The flight is one of the most spectacular anywhere on the canal system, but because of its location on the esoteric BCN it tends to be less celebrated than the likes of Bingley, Foxton and Devizes. On the off-side of the locks a series of overflow weirs cascade spectacularly when water levels are high. When the canal opened in 1779 there were nine locks. The top and bottom are originals, but in 1858 the present central six were built to replace seven earlier locks, traces of which can be explored to the east. A Horseley Iron Works roving bridge spans the original course of the canal below the top lock. In the middle of the flight a former block of canal horse stables is leased to the BCN Society and is occasionally open to the public.

Having acclimatized yourself to the 19th century environs of Black Delph, the next bend in the canal opens out to reveal the 21st century vista of the MERRY HILL CENTRE, one of the new era of out of town shopping developments akin to Sheffield's Meadowhall or the Metro Centre at Gateshead. The canal has recently been slightly

Moorings at Windmill End

TOLL END WORKS

rerouted and one benefit of this work is the provision, at last, of mooring rings for boaters intending to moor up and visit the centre; though many of you will doubtless have taken to the water to escape such manifestations of modern life.

THE WATERFRONT, a billion pound development mixing commerce with leisure, occupies the site of the once vast Round Oak steel works. Aesthetically it is barely an improvement on the past: arguably the most satisfying building of the development is the pub, a pasticed cross between an East Anglian watermill and a Black Country foundry with plenty of mock weatherboarding and reconditioned brick; there must be a moral in that somewhere.

Passing the former junction of the Two Locks Line at Woodside Junction, the canal reaches the 12 feet deep Blower's Green Lock and PARK HEAD JUNCTION. Here the two Dudley Canals met, the No.1 Canal proceeding up the Park Head flight to the portal of DUDLEY TUNNEL. Re-opened in 1992 after a long period of neglect, we were looking forward to researching this route - even if it meant 'legging' the boat through so as avoid making fumes - only to be thwarted by the restricted loading gauge of Dudley Tunnel. Considering that our boat on this occasion was a traditional tug, well-ballasted and tanked full with water to render it as low in the water as possible, we were disappointed to discover that it wouldn't fit. Since then, the Dudley Canal Trust have introduced a tug service (free of charge, though donations are welcome) to haul boats through their Aladdin's Cave of a tunnel; though of course the size limitations still apply. The Trust can be contacted on 01384 236275 for advice and further details, and the more advance warning they get of your intended passage the better. It is rewarding, however, to visit Park Head, if only to admire the handsome pump house - which the Trust have developed as an educational centre - and to take in the canalscene as a whole, and we can recommend mooring here and strolling up to view, not only the southern portal of Dudley Tunnel, but the interesting remains of the Pensnett Canal and Grazebrook Arm as well.

Looking down Parkhead Locks on the Dudley No.1 Canal

Park Head - Windmill End

The Dudley No.2 Canal once totalled eleven route miles, linking the Dudley No.1 Canal at Park Head with the Worcester & Birmingham Canal at Selly Oak (Map 11). It was completed in 1798 and included Britain's fourth longest canal tunnel at Lapal (3795 yards), a daunting towpath-less bore subject to a unique system of operation whereby a steam pumping engine produced an artificial bi-directional current through the tunnel to aid the momentum of boats passing through.

Between Park Head and Windmill End the canal describes a wide arc, clinging to the 453ft contour at the foot of Netherton Hill. Once upon a time industry congregated beside its banks: collieries, claypits, furnaces, limekilns and ironworks. But now this is coot country and the reeds seem as abundant as any Broadland river. At Blackbrook Junction the other end of the Two Locks Line is still evident through its roving bridge, even if subsidence caused it to be abandoned in 1909. We saw an all too rare water vole busily at work here on our last visit. Clothed in gorse and hawthorn, Netherton Hill stands behind the erstwhile junction, climbing to a 600ft summit topped by St Andrew's church where cholera victims are buried in unmarked common graves in the churchyard. The surrounding environs offer generous views over the southern extents of the not so Black Country and the distant wooded tops of the Clent Hills rising to a thousand feet southwards beyond Halesowen; it's a view the west midlands author Francis Brett Young must have known and valued.

A housing estate occupies the site of Doulton's once extensive clay pit linked to the canal by a tramway incline. Boats would carry this clay along the Dudley Canal to the firm's works at Darby End. High Bridge spans a rocky cutting where originally the canal builders built a short-lived tunnel. Nowadays the exhaust from your boat reverberates and rebounds between the sheer sandstone slopes of the cutting. No wonder the old boatmen nicknamed this 'Sounding Bridge'. Lodge Farm reservoir gleams like antimony in its cup of land between the canal and Saltwells Nature Reserve. Footpaths penetrate its hinterland, threading their way through swampy pools down to Cradley Heath.

We've seen elsewhere on the BCN how the railways developed a network of interchange basins and boatage depots. Two of the best preserved examples of this are encountered hereabouts. Primrose Boatage Depot provided the LMS Railway (and its antecedents) with water access to an area otherwise dominated by GWR lines. LMS boats traded between here and the company's interchange basins at Bloomfields (Map 8) and Albion (Map 9). Latterly used by a builders merchant, it seems largely derelict now, though some of the buildings happily remain intact and can be glimpsed over the roving bridge; those with A1 eyesight might even detect the words London Midland & Scottish Railway in faded paint on a gable end. Half a mile away, by Bishtons Bridge, the Great Western Railway's Withymoor Basin was one of the most extensive interchange points between rail and canal in its heyday. Withymoor opened in 1878 and closed in 1965. Its last regular transhipment cargo was chain from Lloyds Proving House by Primrose Bridge. Sadly its transhipment sheds and canopies have been demolished, but its arm survives in water, providing useful residential moorings for the Withymoor Island Trust.

Mention of chain recalls Netherton's landbased involvement in maritime engineering. Did you know that the *Titanic's* anchors were cast here? Each anchor required a team of twenty-four horses to tow it out of Netherton. There was a tradition of chain and anchor making in this unlikely corner of the Black Country. Much of the chain-making was done by women packed tightly in small premises which became so hot that they habitually worked bare-breasted. Would that the Black Country had had an artist of the calibre of Joseph Wright of Derby to do justice to such scenes. The workshops of the new estates which fringe the canal seem nebulous in comparison. Hingley's, owners of Netherton Ironworks, were instrumental in the establishment of Midlands & Coast Canal Carriers following the demise of the Shropshire Union fleet in 1921.

WINDMILL END is arguably the epitome of the Black Country canal scene, and given its location at the centre of the inland waterways system, together with the public open space which lines its canal banks, it's not surprising that it serves from time to time as an ideal venue for major boat rallies. The gaunt outline of Cobb's engine house, silhouetted against the Rowley Hills, above a profusion of Toll End Works roving bridges, forms one of the Black Country's most potent post-industrial images. Would, though, that the 'Bumble Hole' push & pull train still steamed back and forth between Dudley and Old Hill. Admirable as it undoubtedly is, the Visitor Centre (Tel: 01384 814100) is little consolation to connoisseurs of forgotten branch lines; though Windmill End station was immortalised in Flanders & Swann's lovely, and outrageously neglected song *Slow Train*.

Cobb's engine house contained a stationary steam engine which pumped excess water from coal mines in the vicinity and discharged it into the canal. Built in 1831, the engine kept the pits dry and the cut wet for well nigh a century, until the local collieries were all worked out. The engine subsequently went for scrap, but the engine house remains, adorning the landscape as if somehow transmuted from a Cornish cliff top. The old colliery precincts surrounding Windmill End are now known as Warren's Hall Park; a haunted countryside to saunter in, to go roaming in the gloaming in, imagining the pandemonium of its industrial past.

Three cast iron roving bridges span the waterways radiating from Windmill End Junction. Originally the Dudley No.2 Canal ran east to west here, following the course of what became quaintly known as the 'Boshboil' and 'Bumble Hole' arms after the loop was cut off by the improvements of 1858 associated with the opening of Netherton Tunnel. The tunnel's southern portal stands to the north of the junction through the arch of a blue-brick overbridge which carried a colliery tramway.

NETHERTON TUNNEL provokes piquant contrast with Dudley Tunnel's ancient confines. High, wide and equipped with twin towpaths, it now lacks only the lighting once generated by a turbine fed from the high level old main line at Tividale (Map 9). It takes roughly half an hour to walk (preferably with a torch) or boat through this monument to the last fling of the canal age. We counted seven airshafts providing 'air-raids' of rainwater, but we've met wetter tunnels on our canal travels.

Windmill End - Hawne Basin

Lapal Tunnel's closure in 1917 severed the Dudley No.2 Canal's route between Windmill End and Selly Oak, but this end of the canal remained in commercial use right up until 1969 to serve the giant tube making works at Coombeswood on the far side of Gosty Hill Tunnel. Thereafter the canal might easily have deteriorated but for the emergence of the Coombeswood Canal Trust who developed the railway interchange basin at Hawne, on the outskirts of Halesowen, into a flourishing centre of Black Country leisure boating. The journey down to Hawne is continually engrossing if less than edifying. Old basins abound and 19th century large scale maps illuminate the density of industry here.

The canal still narrows at Rowley Stop, but these days no one materialises to take the tolls, so you proceed beneath Hollis's Bridge and on past a roving bridge under which an arm once extended into Old Hill Ironworks. Opposite here, we were gratified to learn, stood Pearson's Colliery, but if we were counting on the shares as part of our inheritance, we are in for a disappointment.

By Powke Lane stands the substantial Rowley Regis crematorium and cemetery and suburban Blackheath occupies the adjacent hillside. At Old Hill (where a pair of good pubs - THE WHARF and THE BOAT - tempt you into tarrying) a series of overbridges pass in quick succession as the canal approaches the stygian delights of GOSTY HILL TUNNEL. In the early years of the 20th century the BCN operated a tug service through the tunnel and the remains of its dock can be seen beside the northern portal. The tunnel's confined, towpathless bore is infamous in boating circles. Working boatmen were content to abandon the tiller and spend the time it took to pass through the 557 yards long tunnel in their boat cabins, whilst, as snugly as a piston in a cylinder, the boat made its own way from one end to another.

You used to emerge from Gosty Hill Tunnel into the eerie precincts of a massive tube works. The canal traversed a canyon of sheer brick walls and passed beneath a sequence of mysterious corrugated iron clad overbridges and pipes whispering loquaciously with escaping steam. Some of the last commercial activity on the area's canals survived here. All this now, however, has vanished and redevelopment is in the air. Beyond the works the canal runs at the foot of Mucklow Hill, a pleasant open landscape threaded by public footpaths. Then, abruptly, comes journey's end in the old transhipment basin at Hawne. Visiting boaters are welcomed but not intruded upon, and this is definitely one Black Country mooring where the nightmare of vandalism won't disturb your slumbers. As to the remainder of the Dudley No.2's route, its future lies in the capable hands of the Lapal Canal Trust - founded in 1990 - torchbearers with a long term interest in restoration of the canal and Lapal Tunnel to their former glory. Recent achievements include the reinstatement of a massive embankment at Leasowes.

B.C.N. Backwaters

Morose and Lugubrious - Walsall Locks

THE Wyrley & Essington is the Jekyll & Hyde of the BCN: at its worst it can be filthy, boring and abused; at best refreshingly remote, unsullied and rural. But in one characteristic it is consistent - it meanders in best contour fashion - hence its nickname:"Curly Wyrley." It opened, independently of the Birmingham Canal, in 1797; extending for 24 miles from Horseley Fields, Wolverhampton to Huddlesford Junction on the Coventry Canal (Map 24) near Lichfield. Its fidelity to the 473ft contour was absolute until Ogley (Map 37) beyond which there were no less than thirty locks in the seven mile stretch down to Huddlesford. Several branches were built, so that by the mid 19th century there were half a dozen or more important junctions adding traffic to what had become a route of much importance. The W&E merged with the BCN in 1840.

It is difficult to be lyrical about the length of canal on this map, but easy to be melancholic. In our experience the sun seldom shines on Wednesfield. Apart from the roving bridge at its erstwhile junction all trace of the Bentley Canal (which linked the W&E with the Walsall Canal at Darlaston (Map 41) seems to have vanished under a retail park development. Postwar maps depict the Curley Wyrley wandering east of Wednesfield through an open countryside broken only by occasional colliery communities, but nowadays the route is bordered by interminable housing. Tedium sets in for the canal traveller and a strange silence hangs over these suburbs, leaving you to speculate what domestic dramas are unfolding inside all these homes with their backs turned so blatantly away from The Cut. At Lane Head the arm which served Holly Bank Colliery basin is still in water, though no longer do the mineral trains come clangorously down from Hilton Main.

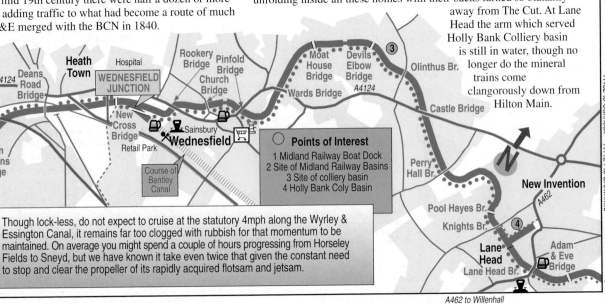

Points of Interest
1 Midland Railway Boat Dock
2 Site of Midland Railway Basins
3 Site of colliery basin
4 Holly Bank Coly Basin

Though lock-less, do not expect to cruise at the statutory 4mph along the Wyrley & Essington Canal, it remains far too clogged with rubbish for that momentum to be maintained. On average you might spend a couple of hours progressing from Horseley Fields to Sneyd, but we have known it take even twice that given the constant need to stop and clear the propeller of its rapidly acquired flotsam and jetsam.

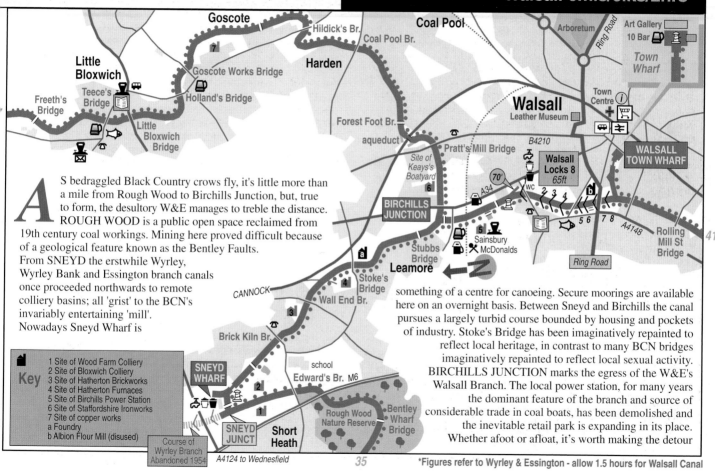

A S bedraggled Black Country crows fly, it's little more than a mile from Rough Wood to Birchills Junction, but, true to form, the desultory W&E manages to treble the distance. ROUGH WOOD is a public open space reclaimed from 19th century coal workings. Mining here proved difficult because of a geological feature known as the Bentley Faults. From SNEYD the erstwhile Wyrley, Wyrley Bank and Essington branch canals once proceeded northwards to remote colliery basins; all 'grist' to the BCN's invariably entertaining 'mill'. Nowadays Sneyd Wharf is something of a centre for canoeing. Secure moorings are available here on an overnight basis. Between Sneyd and Birchills the canal pursues a largely turbid course bounded by housing and pockets of industry. Stoke's Bridge has been imaginatively repainted to reflect local heritage, in contrast to many BCN bridges imaginatively repainted to reflect local sexual activity. BIRCHILLS JUNCTION marks the egress of the W&E's Walsall Branch. The local power station, for many years the dominant feature of the branch and source of considerable trade in coal boats, has been demolished and the inevitable retail park is expanding in its place. Whether afoot or afloat, it's worth making the detour

Key
1 Site of Wood Farm Colliery
2 Site of Bloxwich Colliery
3 Site of Hatherton Brickworks
4 Site of Hatherton Furnaces
5 Site of Birchills Power Station
6 Site of Staffordshire Ironworks
7 Site of copper works
a Foundry
b Albion Flour Mill (disused)

Course of Wyrley Branch Abandoned 1954

*Figures refer to Wyrley & Essington - allow 1.5 hours for Walsall Canal

to the top of the Walsall flight at least. The generating plant brought considerable traffic to the canal. A sizeable unloading basin was serviced by overhead travelling cranes whose grabs lifted considerable tonnages out of fleets of Joey boats.

The Walsall Branch terminated, prior to the construction of the Walsall Junction Canal and its flight of eight locks, at Birchills Wharf. Here, in 1900, a Boatmen's Mission or 'Rest' was built under the aegis of the Incorporated Seamen & Boatmen's Friendly Society. Its function was similar to that at Tipton (Map 8) but at Birchills an upper storey provided considerable dormitory facilities for day boatmen as well. Unfortunately, although the building has been used as a canal museum for a number of years, it has recently had to close due to lack of local authority funding.

Walsall (Locks & Town Arm)

WALSALL LOCKS were first mooted to link the Wyrley & Essington and Walsall canals in 1825, but the W&E and BCN companies were suspicious of each other's motives and proposal was followed by counter-proposal for fifteen years before the canal and its flight of eight locks, rising 65 feet, materialised. The flight seems characteristically morose and lugubrious, as evinced by the crucifix overlooking Lock 5. Alongside Lock 7, fronting Wolverhampton Road, is an impressive flour mill dating from 1849. An arched loading bay covers a side pond beside the lock chamber. Sadly, when we came to visit it researching this edition, we found the mill closed down. Lock 6 is unique to the flight in having mitred bottom gates; the rest being more typical of BCN design with single leaves.

Following many years of decay and dereliction, the WALSALL TOWN ARM has been impressively revitalised, and creates an off-beat gateway to the town's new art gallery; a £21m project designed by Peter St John and Adam Caruso. The gallery's hundred foot high, terracotta-tiled tower forms a fitting new climax to the canal arm. In the far off days of commercial carrying, several basins extended off the arm serving two iron works, the town's original gas works, and the corporation wharf. The Walsall Canal between Walsall and Great Bridge is described in the text accompanying Map 41.

Birchills - Little Bloxwich

Sunken wooden narrowboat hulls lie in the reeds east of Birchills Junction, eloquent testimony to the BCN's busy past. There are no tangible remains, however, of the boat docks which once stood by Pratt's Mill Bridge. Bowaters and Worseys - both famous Black Country boatbuilders - had premises here. In latter years the yard west of the bridge - now covered by housing - was operated by Peter Keay & Son, one of the last specialist wooden canal boat builders. Keays went into business after the Great War, based at first on the Daw End Branch, and were also known as canal carriers by virtue of their fleet of tugs which towed 'Joey' boats down from the Cannock coalfield. Joey was a BCN colloquialism for day boats without living accommodation used for short haul work. Tugs would pull 'trains' of these unpowered craft, or they might be worked singly by horses. They were equipped with transferable helms for bi-directional working, saving the need to turn in space-restricted basins. In fact, the helm was considered part of each boatman's personal tackle, enabling him to effect a rapid change from loaded to empty craft to speed turnrounds.

An aqueduct carries the canal over the Walsall - Cannock revitalised railway. The original course of the canal was by-passed when the railway cutting was excavated, thus allowing the aqueduct to be built without disrupting canal trade. Through Harden, Coal Pool and Little Bloxwich housing estates border the canal. Pilfering was commonplace when the coal boats passed by. Boater captains were apt to turn a blind eye however flagrant the theft. The easiest approach was to board a boat at one bridge-hole, fill a bag with the black stuff, and alight at the next.

Pigeon lofts clutter a significantly high proportion of the canalside gardens, but you don't need us to evoke analogies between the mental imprisonment of their owners and the bird's airborne freedom. Goscote's copper works has bitten the dust and now lilies thrive on the under-boated canal. The appetising aroma of fried batter emanates from a fish & chip shop beside Teece's Bridge. At FREETH'S BRIDGE eastbound canal travellers wriggle free from the suffocation of the suburbs and escape into an open, level countryside which seems doubly beautiful in the light of what has gone before. Paradoxically, the working boatmen of the last century would be passing from farmland into an area of coal mining.

Catshill Junction, Brownhills

THE canals depicted (overleaf) on Map 37 consisted - in their heyday - of the Wyrley & Essington Canal together with seven arms or branches, three of which remain navigable. At Ogley Junction the Wyrley & Essington continued in an easterly direction, skirting Lichfield on its way to join the Coventry Canal at Huddlesford (Map 24). Plans exist to restore this missing link as part of a revived route between the Staffordshire & Worcestershire Canal at Hatherton (Map 31) and Huddlesford. As for the arms and branches, the majority of them: Lord Hays Branch and the Gilpins, Slough and Sandhills arms, are long gone; but the Cannock Extension Canal (or at least a mile and a half of it), the Anglesey Branch and the Daw End Branch remain.

The Cannock Extension Canal

The Cannock Extension Canal opened in 1863 to tap the Cannock coalfield. It was five miles long, lockless, and terminated at Hednesford, a colliery town at the very foot of Cannock Chase. En route there was a junction at Bridgtown, where a precipitous flight of thirteen locks linked with the Hatherton Branch of the Staffs & Worcs Canal. The Cannock Extension was revered as the scene of the 'Black Country Tide', a canal water bore caused by the simultaneous movement of convoys of narrowboats. Perhaps fifty boats at a time would converge on Pelsall Junction from the Walsall and Brownhills directions, and their passage up the Extension would raise the water level by half a foot. Ironically, mining subsidence brought about abandonment of the Cannock Extension above the A5 at Norton Canes in 1963, though by this time the coalfield's dwindling output was mostly railborne in any case.

The Extension was probably the last narrow gauge canal of any significant length to be built, and it has a distinctive character. Even in its decay, it retains a commercial sense of purpose. Blue 'Utopia' engineering bricks line its banks;

continued on page 73

71

Triangle

ANGLESEY BASIN

Chasewater Reservoir

sand pits

Norton Canes

Course of Cannock Extension Canal

Turf Lodge

Course of LNWR Norton Branch

Chasewater Light Railway

Burntwood Rd. Br.

ANGLESEY BRANCH

oil depot

Freeth Bridge

WATLING STREET

Canal Transport Services

70'

WATLING STREET

Little Chef

Toll Road

Beacon Way

aqueduct
Middleton Br.

Anglesey Br.

B4155

Course of Wyrley & Essington to Huddlesford

Staffs

West Mids

Holland Park

Anglesey Bridge Marina

Brownhills Nature Trail

Course of South Staffordshire Railway

OGLEY JUNCT

Key

1 Rems of Brownhills (Grove) Coly.
2 Sites of various collieries
3 Site of iron & spelter works
4 Site of Walsall Wood Coly.
5 Converted flour mill

Engine Lane

Wyrley Common

Course of Mid. Rly Walsall Wood Extension

Becks Bridge

Brownhills

CANNOCK EXTENSION CANAL

Course of Slough Arm

B4154

Wyrley Grove Bridge

Cooper's Bridge

Course of Sandhills Arm

Green Bridge

Jolly Collier Bridge

A452

B5011

Anchor Inn

Pelsall Common Br.

High Bridge

Clayhanger Bridge

P

CATSHILL JUNCTION

Lord Hays Branch

Yorks Br.

A4124

Clayhanger

Shire Oak

60'

Friar Bridge

3

4

Royal Oak

DAW BRANCH

2

2

Pelsall Works Bridge

Free Trade

PELSALL JUNCTION

Yorks Foundry Bridge

4

Points of Interest

1 Valve House
2 Rems of coly basin
3 Site of rly/canal interchange basin
4 Rems of boat horse stables

36

Pelsall   Crse. of Gilpins Arm

38

A461 to Walsall   A452 to Castle Bromwich

N

continued from page 71

BCN concrete fencing posts can be glimpsed in the undergrowth; and hefty, name-plated overbridges - more railway-like than canal - parenthesise its passage across the moody, returning to nature landscape. Two old BCN cottages (No.s 211 & 212) adjoin the massive proportions of Friar Bridge. Opposite are old stables retaining the framework of their stalls. Wasteland extends westwards across Wood Common, a heathery, pock-marked site of a huge ironworks.

Pelsall - Ogley

PELSALL JUNCTION is the scene of occasional boat rallies, but at other times few boats pass by, let alone negotiate the junction and head for Norton Canes. A shame, because this really is a nice place to moor overnight, soaking up the haunted setting of post-industrial inactivity; all fir trees and ponds where once there were slag-heaps and mineral railways. A big public open space encourages the stretching of boating-stiff limbs, whilst hearty appetites can be appeased at one or other (or both) of the adjoining pubs.

East of Pelsall the canal becomes an aquatic corset, keeping the housing estates at bay. Only occasionally does the whalebone burst as urbanisation spills across the cut. The Gilpins and Slough arms were disused by the end of the 19th century; the latter had two locks leading to a short summit fed by local springs and colliery pumping. A public footpath - part of a local nature trail - follows its course now. The defunct "Jolly Collier" inn had stabling for canal horses.

Two abandoned railways crossed the canal either side of Cooper's Bridge. The South Staffordshire line bridge is still in place, its cast iron parapets of exactly the same design as the company's bridge at the foot of the Ryder's Green flight (Map 41). You have to be even older to remember the Midland Railway's Walsall Wood extension in action, the high abutment of its former bridge across the canal provides the lost route with a crumbling memorial.

Twin arms extended into the railway interchange basin at BROWNHILLS and their location is still reasonably evident. A neat brick quayside, irreverently known as 'Brownhills Pier', lures you into mooring up at Brownhills, but in our experience the margins are shallow and long gang-planks a necessity. Clayhanger Common incorporates ninety acres of colliery waste redeveloped as a public open space including a Site of Importance for Nature Conservation. CATSHILL JUNCTION is overlooked by tower blocks. Both routes narrowed here to facilitate toll taking.

The W&E proceeds from Catshill to Ogley passing the long vanished course of the Sandhills Arm, known to working boatmen as the 'Apple Arm' because it traversed an area of orchards. These have gone, but farmland falls bucolically away to the east as the canal enters a shallow cutting of bracken and broom to reach Ogley Junction.

The Anglesey Branch

Chasewater Reservoir was opened in 1800 to supply the Wyrley & Essington main line with much needed water. Fifty years later, with the development of coal mining in the area, the feeder to Ogley was upgraded to navigable standards. Nowadays the branch represents the furthest north you can travel on the BCN. Come this far and you can assume you've won your spurs.

An aqueduct carries the canal over the trackbed of the South Staffordshire Railway. Tom Foxon wrote evocatively of ANGLESEY BASIN in its days as a centre for the loading of coal boats in *No.1*, a classic account of life amongst working boatmen in the early Fifties; notwithstanding that, as publishers, we were forced to 'remainder' it due to poor sales. Tom deserved better, he described how the colliery wagons were upended and their contents carried by conveyor belt to a loading gantry spanning the canal. The gantry consisted of two chutes: one for large lumps of coal which could not be dropped from a great height for fear of damage to the boat holds. Typically the coal would leave in 'trains' of five loaded day boats hauled by a tug, destined perhaps for Birchills power station or the GEC works at Witton. It's a shame that more present day canal users seem unable to bring themselves to find an interest in the past workings of the network. More than anything else, it is paradoxically the past which brings these BCN backwaters alive. You have to imagine them performing the function for which they were built in order to derive the most from their exploration. The last coal was loaded at Anglesey in 1967 and only some contorted lumps of metal recall the existence of such complicated apparatus. The basin is green now, an expanse of water of lake-size proportions considered, in its heathland environment, to be a Site of Special Scientific Interest. Not, naturally, that such status should get in the way of a good old bit of road-building, witness the new Toll Road, what chance a peaceful overnight mooring at Anglesey Basin now?

THE navvies who laboured to build the DAW END BRANCH of the Wyrley & Essington Canal probably wouldn't recognise it now. When it opened in 1800, as a link to the limestone quarries at Hay Head, it was a typical contour canal, crossing a district largely innocent of industry and urbanisation. But it soon became apparent that the hinterland of Brownhills was rich in clay deposits, and brick and tile making became the staple activities of the area. Coal mining prospered too, bequeathing a legacy of subsidence which wrought havoc with the canal bed, necessitating continual heightening of its banks, so that it came to resemble a Fenland river. So it's likely that old-stagers would furrow their brows in amazement to see their cut twisting and turning high above the rest of the crumbling landscape, whilst today's canal travellers find themselves somewhat

burying dangerous wastes in the former clay pits. More memories are evoked at Hopley's Bridge where Duckham's canalside works was the recipient of the ill-fated Birmingham & Midland oil consignments from Ellesmere Port in 1970; perhaps the last long distance narrowboat cargo of note; poignantly, the mooring rings are still there. Two of Walsall MBC's imaginative nature reserves can be found alongside the Daw End Branch: at Park Lime Pits and Hay Head, both sites formerly worked as limestone quarries.

At LONGWOOD the Daw End Branch turned eastwards to reach the limestone workings at Hay Head, and there was no canal link southwards until the merger of the BCN and W&E in 1840. The Rushall Canal was an offspring of this union though, maintaining the connubial metaphor, there is reason to believe that the resultant waterway was by way of being an accident of careless family planning. Apparently the BCN began to have doubts about the viability of the proposed link, only to be reminded that government money borrowed under the Act of Union with the W&E would have to be returned should the Rushall Canal not be built!

voyeuristically at bedroom and bathroom level of houses lining the canal at WALSALL WOOD: some of those wallpapers are hard to take seriously. In Tom Foxon's day Walsall Wood was the location of 'The Traveller', probably the last pub in England to offer stabling for canal horses. The Utopia blue bricks we discovered on the Cannock Extension were apparently made in a canalside works near Northywood Bridge. These days the local industry seems more concerned with

EVEN the most committed BCN diehard would admit that the canals featured on this map hardly represent the system at its most scintillating. Suffocated by suburbia and motorways, unrelievedly straight - and therefore lacking the inherent 'mystery' of the classic winding canal - they lack the dynamism of the industrialised BCN at its best. Such criticisms, though, are relative, and it would be an unimaginative canal explorer who failed to find something, at least, of interest in the characters of these two routes. RUSHALL LOCKS were nicknamed 'The Ganzies' by working boatmen, reputedly because of the thick Guernsey style sweaters favoured by steerers on this windswept cut. In the pound between locks 6 and 7 stood Bell Wharf, one of the few predominantly agricultural basins to be found on the BCN.

Half on embankments, half in cuttings, the TAME VALLEY CANAL's most dramatic incident is its crossing, on an imposing three-arch aqueduct, of the Grand Junction Railway; a rare case (possibly unique) of a railway pre-dating an adjoining canal. We were intrigued by the proliferation - west of Stone Cross - of side bridges. Our trusty 1904 6" Ordnance map showed them to have spanned arms serving sandpits and small collieries. HOLLOWAY BANK BRIDGE carries Telford's Holyhead Turnpike road across the canal at Hill Top. Apparently the road here was so steep that passengers had to climb the hill on foot whilst the horses strained to haul their carriages up unloaded. The region's new Metro system also crosses the canal here, its brightly painted modern trams emphasising the archaic nature of passing boats. Scarcely anything remains of the Balls Hill Branch abandoned in 1960. In typical Brindley fashion a boat would literally have to box the compass when navigating this early waterway. The first cargoes of Wednesbury coal were loaded at its terminus in 1769.

38

Gillity Bridge

3 — Fiveways Bridge

4
Birmingham Rd. Br.

Rushall Locks (9)
65ft 0ins

5
6
7

Bell Br.

8
9

Shustoke Br.

N

Hill Farm Bridge

RUSHALL JUNCTION

Biddleston Bridge

RUSHALL CANAL

M6 Southbound

7

Friar Park Farm Bridge

A4031

M6

Great Barr

Wednesbury Town Centre

school

Crankhall Lane Bridge

aqeducts

R. Tame

M5

sewage works

TAME

park

A4041

playing fields

college

Balls Hill Bridge

Hateley Heath Aqueduct

Metro

Holloway Bank Br.

Stone Cross

TAME VALLEY CANAL

Bishop Ashbury's Cottage

mus

Hill Top

West Bromwich

Course of Balls Hill Branch

The Tame Valley Canal is equipped with towpaths on both of its banks. Generally speaking west of Rushall Junction this is better on the north side, whilst south of Rushall it's better to the west. Tame Bridge railway station provides a useful staging-post for walkers.

Newton Road Bridge
Chimney Bridge

40

75

ONCE upon a time, before the navvies dug this latecomer, the Tame must have been a pretty enough watercourse, skipping gaily down off the Black Country ridge to its confluence with the Trent above Tamworth. Not that the canal can be blamed for the urbanisation of the valley. Save for Hamstead Colliery (whose basin by Gorse Farm Bridge was linked by tramway to the pit head) the Tame Valley Canal attracted little industry to its banks hereabouts, being built primarily - and remaining useful throughout its commercial life - as a by-pass route, enabling through traffics to avoid the centre of Birmingham. No, these fields were filled by the phenomenon of the housing estate which, from the late Thirties onwards, crept northwards from burgeoning Birmingham, creating subtopias out of Perry Barr, Witton and Hamstead. Fortunately, all these Englishmen's castles fail to smother the canal which, either hides in rocky, wooded cuttings reminiscent of 'The Shroppie', or rides upon embankments with views southwards over the Second City. From here it doesn't look far - but it's the best part of a day's boating away!

Two aqueducts of differing design carry the canal above the rooftops of HAMSTEAD. The local colliery closed in the early Sixties. In 1908 there was an underground fire at the pit which claimed the lives of twenty-five miners. One of the trapped groups, anticipating their doom, chalked their names

on a nearby door together with the poignant inscription: "The Lord preserve us for we are all trusting in Christ." Rescue teams with special breathing apparatus were sent from the Yorkshire coalfield, and one of these men, John Welsby, lost his own life, heroically searching for the trapped men. He is commemorated by a street named after him on the estate which now covers the site of the mine.

PERRY BARR LOCKS - colloquially known as the 'New Thirteen' (as opposed to the 'Old Thirteen' at Farmers Bridge (Map 20) - lie adjacent to Perry Park with its impressive athletics stadium. The chambers are fitted with double bottom gates throughout. Interesting relics of the recirculating pumping system, which returned water lost through lock-usage to the top of the flight, are still to be seen: the 'Grid House' at the foot of Lock 13; 'No.1 Reflux Valve' by Lock 11; 'No.2 Reflux Valve' by Lock 7; and the 'Gauging Weir House' at the top of the flight. By the time the foot of the flight has been reached, the canal finds itself re-entering Birmingham's industrial zone. Travelling southbound, the suburban dream is over.

"*T*HE time to explore these lugubrious waters - these Cinderella canals which constitute the northern sections of the BCN - is now, while they are at the nadir of their fortunes. Change is imminent, long overdue, and to be welcomed. But decay, like old age, has a way of tugging at your heart strings, as if there were some mute urgency in disintegration to escape the parameters of time."

That was how we saw the Walsall Canal and its near neighbours in 1989. Over ten years later our predictions prove sadly true. The Black Country Spine Road accompanies the Walsall Canal for much of its length now, and virtually all the old, 'haunted' ambience of the canal has been eradicated with linear development schemes triggered by the advent of the 'trail-blazing' road, likened to a

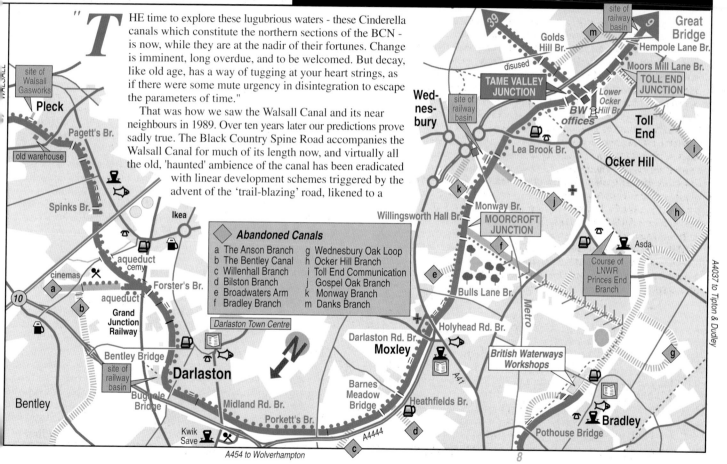

Abandoned Canals

a The Anson Branch	g Wednesbury Oak Loop
b The Bentley Canal	h Ocker Hill Branch
c Willenhall Branch	i Toll End Communication
d Bilston Branch	j Gospel Oak Branch
e Broadwaters Arm	k Monway Branch
f Bradley Branch	m Danks Branch

Roman Road by the Black Country Development Corporation's propaganda in its conceived capacity to create order out of chaos. And so the Walsall Canal of the twenty-first century will assume a cosmetic role within a regenerated zone of business parks, housing schemes, and retail centres. All good clean fun, though just a bit too clean, one suspects, for it to any longer pump the adrenalin of canal enthusiasts, or at least those who have tended to enjoy it latterly in all the glory of its post-industrial decay. The towpath is well-surfaced - presumably the canal will be dredged and cleared of the eclectic floating debris without which no BCN cruise wins its stripes - its banks are becoming overlooked by neat houses, and the threat of hooliganism recedes. But - and to our mind it's a 'Big Woolwich Butty' of a but - what dyed-in-the-wool canal buff, used to getting off on the fantasies of carrying coke to Coseley and tripe to Tipton, is going to derive any satisfaction from walking or boating along a concrete-banked waterway threading its way through housing estates and retail parks and accompanied by a dual-carriageway? Yes chums, we've come to bury the Walsall Canal, not to praise it.

Bearing generally southwards from Walsall - generally, that is, in the context of a contour canal - the Walsall runs through the suburb of Pleck, passing the site of Walsall gasworks, a relatively late user of canal transport; coal in and waste products out. In fact, Thomas Clayton's very last run was from here with crude tar to Oldbury on 31st March, 1966 aboard the motor boat *Stour*. The canal slips through Pleck in a sandy cutting and then passes beneath an office block adjoining James Bridge copper works. Emerging from beneath the M6 motorway it rides upon a considerable embankment carrying it over a by-road and the infant River Tame. To the north-west other lofty earthworks can be seen. This was the Anson Branch - still partially in water - which connected with the Bentley Canal abandoned in 1961 (Map 35).

The canal crosses the Grand Junction Railway and essays a loop around the old metal-bashing town of Darlaston. Judging by the environs it seems as if the town's boom industry now is demolition. By Bughole Bridge the Spine Road makes itself known to southbound canal travellers for the first time. You are not expected to become bosom pals. The Willenhall and Bilston 'branches' of the canal were little more than glorified basins,

both disused around the end of the 19th century. Likewise the Broadwaters Arm on the far side of Moxley. Redevelopment has eroded much of the latent atmosphere of the canal as it reaches MOORCROFT JUNCTION. Until its closure in 1961, the Bradley Branch lead off from here to the Wednesbury Oak Loop, ascending to the Wolverhampton Level through a flight of nine locks. A footpath follows the course of this interesting route under the Metro tramway and up into a public open space circling housing estates to Bradley itself.

The Monway Branch which once served a complex of iron and chemical plants, including the vast Patent Shaft Steel Works. The Gospel Oak branch led to Willingsworth furnaces. Opposite its reedy remains, shot like a green arrow into the entrails of a housing estate, a roving bridge spans the entrance to the Great Western Railway's Wednesbury rail/canal interchange basin.

British Waterways smart new office and visitor centre overlooks TAME VALLEY JUNCTION, from which the canal of the same name egresses eastwards, offering alternative routes to Brownhills and Birmingham. The Lower Ocker Hill Branch was opened in 1785 to feed water to pumping engines at Ocker Hill via a tunnel in the hillside. It remains in water for a few hundred yards and provides useful moorings. To the south another through route has been lost. The Tipton Green & Toll End Communication Canal doesn't exactly roll off the tongue, but until 1960 it 'communicated' with the main line at Tipton, easing congestion in the heyday of the BCN when boats were apt to be choc-a-bloc at Ryders Green. You can walk its course as far as the A461, beyond which it is fenced off.

Alan Godfrey's reprint of the 1902 Ordnance Survey Map for Great Bridge & Toll End depicts in all its fascinating complexity the stretch of canal between Toll End Junction and Ryders Green Bottom Lock. Here the Danks Branch made its dog-leg connection with the Tame Valley Canal, whilst the South Staffordshire Railway spanned the Walsall's main line. It still does (though its tracks haven't seen a train in years - and await the clarion call to become part of the Metro system, linking Walsall with Dudley) but virtually all trace of the extensive London & North Western rail/canal interchange basins have vanished into a swampy undergrowth abutting the Spine Road. *Memento Mori:* all one can do is breath a deep sigh and seek solace in the shape of a Firkin's synthetic cream slice.

A helping hand, Ryders Green flight, Great Bridge

ALVECHURCH *Map 13*

The 'village' lies some distance downhill from the canal. It offers a good range of shops plus fish & chips; but, typically in this age, no longer a bank. Canalside by Bridge 61 stands THE CROWN, an attractively unspoilt little local offering bar meals at most times. Alternatively try THE WEIGHBRIDGE, a boater's club open to non-members at Alvechurch Boat Centres' yard by Bridge 60. Here, also, you'll find an excellently stocked canal shop together with a useful supply of emergency provisions.

TRAINS - half-hourly locals to/from Redditch & Birmingham.
Tel: 0121-200 2700

ARMITAGE *Map 26*

Guide books point to the 'interesting' church perched on a rocky bluff above the bosky canal by Bridge 61, but the village is dominated by the sanitaryware works. There are a number of shops on the main road, but mooring can be problematical on what is a rather narrow and tortuous section of canal. A couple of eating establishments vie for your custom: the PLUM PUDDING (Bridge 61a) has dropped considerably below the level of the canal because of subsidence, but the outdoor patio remains commensurate with the canal; its food is award-winning and accommodation is also available - Tel: 01543 490330. Across the road you could try SPODE COTTAGE, a 'Mighty Nice Pub' housed in a 17th century farmhouse. Tel: 01543 490353. The ASH TREE (Bridge 62) was closed for refurbishment as we went to press following a major fire.

BIRMINGHAM *Maps 11 & 20*

Canal boating holidays come low enough in the kudos stakes, and Birmingham as a destination lower still. But any sympathy your friends can muster will be wasted. Let them bake on some beach. There is more character in Birmingham's big toe than the whole of 'The Med' put together. The city centre is only a brief stroll from the visitor moorings radiating from Old Turn Junction, and its sophisticated character and traffic-free thoroughfares may surprise those with preconceived notions of an ungainly, uncouth city where everyone speaks through its nose and has something to do with the motor trade. But cars have lost their pole position in 'Brummagem's' scheme of things and the city continues to recover from its crass submission to traffic which ruined it a generation ago. Centenary, Chamberlain and Victoria squares set the tone for the canal travellers' perambulation of the city. The first revitalised with the opening of the Convention Centre in 1991, the other two dominated by imposing Victoriana, including the Art Gallery and the Town Hall. There are deeper oases of calm and character to be discovered too. Churches like St Philip's Cathedral and St Paul's (the 'Jeweller's Church'), the bustling markets of the rebuilt Bull Ring, and the quiet backwaters of the Jewellery Quarter. These are the bits of Birmingham you should make it your business to see.

Pubs, restaurants and wine bars gather around the canal between Old Turn and Gas Street like wasps on a cream bun, drawing inspiration from the verisimilitude of the setting and bearing suitably utilitarian names like THE WHARF, THE BRASSHOUSE, THE MALT HOUSE , JAMES BRINDLEY and THE GLASS WORKS , though not - in our opinion - providing the kind of ambience that most conservative canal folk are likely to warm to after a hard day's boating; these are the very places many of you will have taken to the water to escape from! But in Brindley Place and The Mailbox a wider choice of cosmopolitan restaurants has developed where the atmosphere is somewhat less frenetically youth orientated. Try LE PETIT BLANC (Tel: 0121 633 7333) or CAFE IKON (Tel: 0121 248 3226) overlooking Oozells Square; ZIZZI (Tel: 0121 632 1333), DENIAL (Tel: 0121 632 1232) or MALMAISON (Tel: 0121 246 5000) on Wharfside Street in The Mailbox; or the BANK restaurant bar (Tel: 0121 633 4466), CAFE ROUGE (Tel: 0121 643 6556), or TIN TIN Cantonese restaurant (Tel: 0121 633 0888) in Brindleyplace. Two pubs in the vicinity are: THE PRINCE OF WALES, which provides the authenticity of a traditional city centre ale house; and the FLAPPER & FIRKIN at Cambrian Wharf.

continued on page 81

continued from page 80

As something of an antidote to all this sophistication, the CANALSIDE CAFE at Gas Street Basin exudes considerable charm. Finally, if you like eating Spanish, we can recommend LOS CANARIOS (Tel: 0121 236 3495) on Albert Street within easy reach of the Digbeth Branch.

The Bull Ring Shopping Centre - a painful lesson in the excesses of concrete architecture dating from the Sixties - has been redeveloped and 'sexed-up' with a new name - *Bullring*! The landmark Rotunda has escaped by the skin of its Grade II listed teeth, so that it now rubs shoulders with the likes of Kaplicky's shimmering Selfridges store. Two department stores and a hundred and thirty-two shops should keep the womenfolk engaged long enough for a cup-tie at St Andrews or Villa Park, and possibly the replay too.

THE PALLASADES (above New Street Station) and THE PAVILIONS development in High Street are predictable precincts. New Street and Corporation Street burgeon with department stores and multiple chains. Canallers in a hurry - if that's not a contradiction in terms - will find a useful general store adjacent to Tindal Bridge by Farmer's Bridge Junction.

TOURIST INFORMATION - City Arcade (off Corporation St) Tel: 0121 202 5099. Branch desk at International Convention Centre. INTERNATIONAL CONVENTION CENTRE - Broad Street. Tel: 0121 200 2000. Even if you are not a delegate, worth visiting to admire its confident new architecture, or perhaps to enjoy a concert in the splendid SYMPHONY HALL whose Box Office is on 0121 780 3333.
INDOOR ARENA - King Edward's Road. Tel: 0121 200 2202. Sports events, concerts etc.
NATIONAL SEA LIFE CENTRE - Brindley Place. Tel: 0121 633 4700. Fish & stuff!
IKON GALLERY - Oozells Sq, Brindley Place. Tel: 0121 248 0708. Contemporary art venue.
MUSEUM & ART GALLERY - Chamberlain Square. Open daily, admission free. Recently boosted by opening of Gas Hall extension. Rivals Manchester in the richness of its PreRaphaelite collection.Tel: 0121 303 2834.
MUSEUM OF THE JEWELLERY QUARTER - Vyse Street (Hockley). Open Mon-Sat. Quarter of an hour's walk from Farmer's Bridge but well signposted. Open Mon-Sat. Tel: 0121 554 3598. Housed in former jewellery factory. Shop & refreshments.
THINKTANK - Curzon Street. Tel: 0121 202 2222. Science can be fun! New home to Watt's Smethwick Engine and Stanier's *City of Birmingham*.
BOAT TRIPS - several operators: Second City 0121 236 9811; Parties Afloat 0121 236 7057; Canal Leisure Services 0121 507 0477; and Sherborne Wharf

0121 455 6163.
Local bus & train hotline: 0121 200 2700.
Nationwide trains: 08457 484950.

BROMSGROVE *Map 14*

Being two or three miles west of Tardebigge (though the station and a useful selection of shops, including Banners excellent food store, are at Aston Fields) Bromsgrove lies outside the orbit of most canal travellers. But it's an attractive, old-fashioned sort of town which glories in its connections with A.E. Housman (the poet, whose statue adorns the pedestrianised High Street) and the celebrated 'Bromsgrove Guild' founded in 1894 as a federation of local craftsmen. There are buses from Tardebigge or Aston Fields. Further information from the MUSEUM & TOURIST INFORMATION CENTRE on Birmingham Road. Tel: 01527 831809.

BROWNHILLS *Map 37*

The long main street is typical of its era, the lacklustre shop frontages harbouring no ambitions above the monotony of two storeys; a rash of nonconformist chapels providing all the entertainment the Calvinist inhabitants of Brownhills were ever likely to admit to. And yet, on Tuesdays and Saturdays the canalside market throbs with activity, the car parks are crammed and buses packed with people who you would have thought more plausibly to have done their business in Walsall or Cannock. Tesco supermarket adjacent canal; various banks.

COOKLEY *Map 3*

A village with an iron-making tradition going back three centuries. There are two pubs and a fish & chip shop, whilst a post office stores (open daily EC Wed & Sun) butcher, supermarket (with cash machine) and newsagent make Cookley a useful and friendly port of call for the day's provisions.

COSELEY *Map 8*

Possibly useful provisioning point between Wolverhampton and Tipton, but no really decent moorings, whilst the shops themselves are located on the brow of a hill above the tunnel. Some of the local pubs supplied by local brewer Holdens of Woodsetton, arguably the most satisfying (and certainly one of the cheapest) Black Country ales.

COVEN *Map 32*

The village lies ten minutes walk from Bridge 71. Be mindful of the A449's traffic. Facilities include a post office, general store, grocer, butcher, bakery, newsagent and fish & chip shop. Canalside you'll find THE FOX & ANCHOR. Tel: 01902 798786. There's an hourly bus service to/from Wolverhampton.

CURDWORTH *Map 22*

The village street is reached by crossing the busy A4079. Curdworth is one of several Warwickshire villages purporting to be at the centre of England. It is also one of the oldest settlements in this part of the world and gets its name from Crida, the first King of Mercia. Facilities include a post office stores (EC Tue & Sun) and two pubs, one of which, the WHITE HORSE (Tel: 01675 470227), is canalside.

DROITWICH *Map 15*

In common with Bromsgrove, Droitwich is probably too far from the canal for the average traveller to bother visiting. It's perhaps the best part of half an hour's walk to the town centre from Hanbury Wharf, where the EAGLE & SUN pub sees to immediate needs. Towpath walkers, however, may find it necessary to trudge along the Salt Road in order to make their way to or from the station. If you do bother to visit it, you'll find a likeable town with the air of a spa about it. Further information from the TOURIST INFORMATION & HERITAGE CENTRE (an admirable little museum featuring the history of the town's salt trade as well as the background to nearby Wychbold radio transmitting station) on 01905 774312.

DUNHAMPSTEAD *Map 16*

Hamlet which gains an entry in the gazetteer by virtue of THE FIRS INN (Tel: 01905 774094) a pretty and comfortable country pub offering excellent food and a decent choice of beers. Also adjacent to Bridge 30 you'll find FORGE STUDIO, a canal craft shop.

FAZELEY *Map 23*

Now by-passed by the A5, Fazeley seems somewhat less frenetic than in the past, and there are useful facilities in what, because of its junction status, has always been a popular overnight mooring point. Those facilities include a couple of pubs, a fish & chip shop and an Indian restaurant called the IVORY TUSK - Tel: 01827 285777. There's a general store, butcher, newsagent, post office and off licence. For banks etc, you'll have to catch the bus into nearby Tamworth.

DRAYTON MANOR PARK - open daily Easter to October. Admission charge. Access on A4091 adjacent to Drayton footbridge. Tel: 01827 287979. Family theme park, amusements, zoo, farm park, nature trail and woodland walks.

GREAT BRIDGE *Map 9*

The Spine Road has brought 21st century reality to Great Bridge - there are even KFC and McDonalds 'drive-thrus' - and we were saddened to see the exorcism of much of the town's time-warp atmosphere so prevalent when we last journeyed this way. Still, the West Bromwich Building Society continues to advertise itself ingenuously as 'the home of thrift' whilst Great Bridge remains a more than useful frontier post for stocking up on life's little necessities (Tunnocks caramel wafers for example) before heading off into the northern wastes of the BCN.

THE EIGHT LOCKS - canalside top of Ryder's Green Locks. Food, pool, darts and a garden. Fish & chips from THE BLACK COUNTRY CHIPPY. McDONALDS and KFC outlets adjacent Lock 8.

Access between locks 7 and 8 to main thoroughfare of shops including: Barclays bank, Kwik Save and Firkins, famous for their imitation cream slices. ASDA supermarket adjacent Lock 7.

HANDSACRE *Map 26*

MICHAEL'S fish & chip shop (adjacent bridge 58) really is excellent as the queues testify. Also worthy of a halt is THE CROWN, a congenial local where the locals' repartee is apt to be as frothy as your pint of Bass.

HAYWOODS (GREAT & LITTLE) *Map 28*

The villages of Great and Little Haywood are separated by the long, high brick wall of the Shugborough estate. Dormitory housing has inevitably expanded both populations, but the centres remain peaceful and largely unspoilt; especially so in the charming lane leading from Great Haywood, under the railway and over the canal, to the Essex Bridge, one of the finest examples of a packhorse bridge imaginable. Tolkien once lived in the village.

LOCK HOUSE - adjacent Haywood Lock. Popular tea rooms and licensed restaurant. A pair of pubs in either village.

Little Haywood has a post office stores and a newsagent. Great Haywood has two general stores, a post office, and a farm shop alongside the junction.

SHUGBOROUGH - access via Haywood Lock and Essex Bridge. Open daily April to December. Admission charge. Attractions include mansion, county museum, working farm, gardens, National Trust shop and cafeteria. A visit to the farm can be particularly recommended for families. Frequent special events and a regular point of departure for hot air balloons. Tel: 01889 881388.

BUSES - regular service through Little Haywood to Stafford useful for one-way towpath walks. Tel: 0870 608 2 608.

HOLT FLEET *Map 19*

Good place to stop on the Severn: a pub, a restaurant, and a general store. The pretty village of Ombersley lies 2 miles to the east.

KIDDERMINSTER *Map 2*

Famous for its carpets, its steam railway and its football team, 'The Harriers', Kidderminster is a working town with a definite, though difficult to define, appeal. A busy ring road divorces the canal from the town centre, but in the pedestrianised streets the roar of traffic soon dies down, and you can admire 'Kidder's' knack of remembering its most famous sons in statue form.

THE WATERMILL - Bridge 13. Pleasant modern family pub, food and moorings.

KING & CASTLE - Comberton Hill. Instant nostalgia in the Severn Valley Railway's refreshment room. Guest beers and home made food. Tel: 01562 747505. *McDonalds and Pizza Hut by Bridge 16.*

The shopping centre is lively and traffic free. There's a retail market on Thursdays and Saturdays. Sainsbury supermarket canalside above Kidderminster Lock.

TOURIST INFORMATION - Market Street. Tel: 01562 512900.

SEVERN VALLEY RAILWAY - One of Britain's premier preserved railways, the SVR runs up the valley to the Shropshire market town of Bridgnorth, a delightful ride in its own right, never mind the fun of being hauled by steam. Services run throughout the summer and on most other weekends and holiday periods. Talking timetable on 01299 401001.

BUSES - Midland Red West services. Tel: 0870 608 2 608. Useful links with Stourport for towpath walkers.

TRAINS - frequent local services to/from Birmingham and Worcester etc. Tel: 08457 484950.

KINVER *Map 3*

Kinver is well aware of its charms and flaunts them to the full. Visitors pour in during the summer months, filling car-parks at the rear of the pubs, restaurants and cafes which provide most of the fabric of High Street. But somehow Kinver preserves its appeal and repays the ten minute stroll from the canal. In any case, the village's main asset is its superb setting in the shadow of Kinver Edge, a dramatic wooded ridge rising to five hundred feet and the southern end of the 'Staffordshire Way' long distance footpath. For those with time and energy at their disposal, the climb to the top of The Edge can be recommended. On a clear day you can see - well almost, as the song says, forever - certainly over to Bredon Hill and The Cotswolds.

VINE INN - canalside Bridge 29. Cosy waterside pub offering M&B and guest beers. Nice garden with lots of children's activities.

PLOUGH & HARROW - High Street. Unprepossessing 'local' worth patronising for the medal-winning Batham ales.

THE ANCHOR HOTEL - Dark Lane. Accessible from Bridge 28. Tel: 01384 872085. Snug and friendly little establishment dating from 1410. Kinver boasts many other eating & drinking establishments, from modest cafes to expensive restaurants.

Continued on page 84

Continued from page 83

All the shops (and there's a good choice for such an otherwise small village) congregate along the main street. Galleries and gift shops rub shoulders with a pair of 'Early-Late' shops. Barclays *still* have a small branch bank here with a cash machine.

i TOURIST INFORMATION - Just Petals, High Street. Tel: 01384 877756.

BUSES - successor to the light railway, but not half as romantic, there is an hourly bus link with Stourbridge, Merry Hill and Cradley Heath. Tel: 0121 236 8313.

LANGLEY *Map 9*

Like Great Bridge, Langley seems less of a throw-back than when we first got to know it in the 1980s - though the continued existence of an old-fashioned cobblers does hint at some degree of reluctance to let go the past. We missed the earth-moving thump of Hughes Johnson's foundry presses. But Langley remains a handy stopping point for those intrepid enough to explore the Titford Canal, and lots of nice little shops cater for most needs.

FININGS & FIRKIN - canalside Langley Green Bridge. Formerly known as the Brewery Inn, but still a pleasant stopover.

MERRY HILL *Map 34*

Of course Merry Hill is really Brierley Hill, but so much does the massive retail complex dominate the vicinity now, that it seems more appropriate to refer to it thus. In common with its peers - Meadowhall, Metro, Trafford Park and Thurrock - you either love this sort of thing or loathe it. "Over 200 shops and stores" shrieks the publicity blurb: "two and a half miles of marbled halls - a uniquely enjoyable experience" - much like the BCN itself you might justifiably retort!

BREWER'S WHARF - canalside Green's Bridge. Banks's pub and 'Milestone' restaurant looking faintly ludicrous in its high-tech surroundings, but we dined here one Sunday evening (when all the Waterfront's other restaurants - Indian, Chinese, Greek and Italian - were shut) and thoroughly enjoyed our meal.

THE VINE - better known as the 'Bull & Bladder', Batham's brewery tap is one of the great Black Country pubs. It stands on Delph Road about 5 minutes walk east from the foot of Delph Locks. Lunches, families welcome and, of course Batham's wonderful, wonderful beer which the family have been brewing for five generations. The Vine, one of only nine tied houses, has a Shakespearian quotation emblazoned across its frontage at roof level. Several other pubs congregate on Delph Road: THE DOCK & IRON, BLACK HORSE (Enville Ales), TENTH LOCK and THE BELL but the Bull & Bladder is by far the most atmospheric.

If the prospect of Merry Hill's two hundred plus shops is more than you can bear, then head in the opposite direction for Brierley Hill's beleaguered but traditional High Street. Note also the existence of a UCI Multiscreen cinema adjacent to the canal south of Green's Bridge.

BUSES - but no trains - connect Merry Hill with every conceivable Black Country town.

MILFORD *Map 28*

A motorist's gateway to Shugborough and The Chase unlikely to hold too much attraction for canal travellers. Throughout the summer its 'village green' is covered with parked cars. Facilities, however, include a steak bar, fast food outlet, post office store, newsagent and farm shop. Access from either Bridge 105 or 106.

MINWORTH *Map 21*

A pleasant enough suburb on the edge of the West Midlands conurbation with a handful of useful shops bordering its green, Minworth is known chiefly for the huge sewage works which once boasted an internal narrow-gauge railway system, remains of which can be seen on the road to Water Orton, worth walking to see the magnificent, 6-arch packhorse bridge which has

continued on page 85

Continued from page 84

spanned the Tame since the 16th century.

🫖 THE BOAT - small Ansells pub near Dicken's Bridge advertising Indian cuisine to eat in or take-away . Tel: 0121 240 9696.

THE KINGSLEY - canalside by Wigginshill Road Bridge. Modern pub/steak bar on the county boundary where urbanisation and countryside collide.

NETHERTON *Map 34*

Netherton was literally and metaphorically built on coal. The parish church of St Andrews stands 600ft above sea level on a bare hillside once extensively mined. From its summit there are views across the intervening valley, traversed by the Dudley Canal, to Brierley Hill and the distant horizon of The Wrekin. The sturdy church itself, surrounded by tombstones which tell their own Black Country story of industrial triumph and personal misery, was locked, but we could see that it contained a gallery supported by cast iron columns as well as some interesting stained glass.

🫖 The lamentable demise of Colm & Sheena O'Rourke's 'Little Pubs' has taken the wind out of the sails of their eccentric creations. Most of the pubs themselves, like THE DRY DOCK (Tel: 01384 235369) here at Windmill End, have passed into alternative ownership. Happily, The Dry Dock retains its bar, fashioned from the hull of a former 'Runcorn' narrowboat, and continues to serve Desperate Dan Cow Pie, faggots & peas and other Black Country delicacies, so not all is lost.

♟ Netherton's shops are looking a bit sorry for themselves these days; fed up, no doubt, of competing with Merry Hill. But morale boosting cakes are still obtainable from FIRKINS the West Bromwich bakers, whilst ALLANS discount store remains worth visiting: "every seasonable line imaginable - no nonsense prices." Meanwhile, no self-respecting cowpoke would miss the chance to visit the RANCH HOUSE Western Store - "complete Western & Line Dance outfitters."

ⓘ BUMBLE HOLE VISITOR CENTRE - Tel: 01384 814100. Interesting and friendly centre devoted to Windmill end and its environs.

🚌 BUSES -frequent services to/from Dudley etc. Nearest railway station at Old Hill. Tel: 0121 200 2700.

OLDBURY *Map 9*

Redevelopment continues to alter the face of Oldbury, though here and there echoes of the old Worcestershire town bounce back at you. L.T.C. Rolt wrote:

"Of Oldbury, with its mean, blackened streets, I can find no redeeming word to say," but then he had a horror of over industrialisation, whereas a lot of us have an acute nostalgia for many aspects of it now. The vast conglomerate offices of Sandwell MBC's civic headquarters dominate the town now, and the mind can only boggle at the army of bureaucrats employed in keeping tabs on the rest of us who actually have to make something useful in order to eke out a living.

🫖 WAGGON & HORSES - Church Street. Standing defiantly opposite the civic offices, this CAMRA recommended pub has retained virtually all its Victorian character, right down (or should that be up) to a copper-panelled ceiling! Dispenses many of the region's best local ales plus a cycle of other guest beers. Food usually available Mon-Fri. 5 minutes walk from Whimsey Bridge on the old main line. Tel: 0121 552 5467.

McDONALDS - 'drive-thru' outlet adjacent Whimsey Bridge, though no loop provided for the boat trade as yet.

♟ The best canalside choice in shops between Wolverhampton and Birmingham. The centre is most easily reached from the old main line, but is also little more than half a mile from Telford's route at Bromford. Big Co-op supermarket near Whimsey Bridge, branches of most banks and a small market on Tues & Sats. Some good Black Country butchers and bakers.

🚌 BUSES - bus station adjacent to Whimsey Bridge with information office and frequent departures and arrivals from all over the Black Country. Tel: 0121 200 2700.

TRAINS - InterCity and local services from Sandwell & Dudley railhead by Bromford Bridge. Tel: 08457 484950.

PENKRIDGE *Map 30*

Quite easily the best place to break your journey on the northern section of the Staffs & Worcs. Five minutes walk from the wharf will take you to the narrow main street, a pleasant spot to shop and saunter. At its foot stands an impressive church of sandstone, formerly a collegiate church, considered second only to a cathedral in ecclesiastical status.

🫖 CROSS KEYS - canalside Bridge 84. A once isolated pub, described by Rolt in *Narrow Boat*, but now surrounded by a housing estate, though that doesn't diminish its popularity with boaters.

Continued on page 86

Gazetteer P-S

Gazetteer P-S

continued from page 85

THE BOAT - canalside Bridge 86. Attractively refurbished pub overlooking wharf and Penkridge Lock. Home-cooking. Other pubs worth considering in the centre include The Star, Littleton Arms and The Railway.

Some lovely little shops of character, plus a small supermarket. Lloyds and Barclays banks on A449. Thriving outdoor market on Wednesdays and Sundays beside the river.

BUSES - to Cannock, Wolverhampton and Stafford. Tel: 01543 577099.

TRAINS - to Wolverhampton and Stafford. Tel: 08457 484950.

RUGELEY Map 27

A thousand jobs were lost when Lea Hall's modern colliery closed in 1990. But this is a resilient little town, well versed in the vicissitudes of existence, life here being lived on the cheap, though with a certain deadpan dignity. Here in the tight-knit streets, and on the old Coal Board estates, are thrift and graft and a perverse civic pride, whilst a consoling beauty is to be found up on the nearby Chase.

GEORGE & BERTIES - Albion Street. An unusual cafe with a central bar around which customers sit perched on high stools as if this were somewhere in Belgium. Tel: 01889 577071.

LA TERRAZZA - Italian restaurant housed in an old chapel on Lichfield Street. Tel: 01889 570630.

Moor north of Bridge 66 for easiest access to town centre. Large Safeway supermarket nearby. Market on Tue, Thur-Sat. Most banks and lots of good cake shops.

BUSES - services throughout the Trent Valley and Cannock Chase. If you have time to spare, take the Green Bus to Cannock, a magical mystery tour up and over The Chase. Tel: 01785 223344.

TRAINS - two stations (Town and Trent Valley) support an hourly weekday service between Stafford, Walsall and Birmingham. Tel: 08457 484950.

RUSHALL Map 38

Useful shops and a McDonalds five minutes walk west of Daw End Bridge.

MANOR ARMS - classic canalside pub south of Daw End Bridge. Tradtional interior, lunchtime food; plus evenings Wed-Sat. Nice garden.

SMETHWICK Map10

High Street was sliced in half to make room for the expressway. What remains is more Asian than Anglo-Saxon, but all the more intriguing for that. If you enjoy cooking Indian then this is the place to stop for authentic ingredients; the sweet shops are mouthwatering! Otherwise Smethwick's attractions lie very much in the past, and anyone with an interest in canals and/or industrial archaeology will revel in the panoramic sweep of Brindley's and Telford's split level canals.

GALTON VALLEY CANAL HERITAGE CENTRE - Brasshouse Lane. Tel: 0121 558 8195. Former pub converted to display exhibits and interpretive material relating to Smethwick's fascinating canal history. Access at most times to the adjoining pumphouse. Guided tours arranged for parties booking in advance.

TRAINS - frequent services between Rolfe Street station and Birmingham New Street and between Galton Bridge and Snow Hill. Tel: 0121 200 2700.

STAFFORD Map 29

One of England's lesser-known county towns, Stafford has always seemed too self-effacing for its own good; though there are signs that in recent years it has begun to wake up to its tourist potential. Unfortunately for canal folk, the centre lies over a mile from Radford Bridge. But there are frequent buses, and those with time at their disposal will find Stafford a rewarding place to visit. First stop should be the Ancient High House in Greengate Street - the main thoroughfare. Dating from 1595, it's thought to be the largest timber-framed town house remaining in England. Inside there's a heritage exhibition tracing

continued on page 87

continued from page 86

Stafford's history since 913 when Ethelfleda, daughter of Alfred the Great, fortified the settlement against marauding Danish invaders. King Charles I stayed at High House in 1642, and in later years Izaak Walton visited relatives who owned it. Tel: 01785 619130. A town trail leaflet is available from the TIC to guide you around the best of Stafford's surprisingly rich roll-call of historic buildings.

RADFORD BANK - canalside Bridge 98. Refurbished steak bar. Tel: 01785 242825.

THE MOAT HOUSE - canalside Bridge 92, Acton Trussell. Four star hotel in former moated farmhouse: restaurant and bars, lovely gardens, customer moorings. Tel: 01785 712217.

THE SOUP KITCHEN - Church Lane. Quaint and bustling eatery serving coffees, lunches and teas. Tel: 01785 254775.

STAFFORD ARMS - Railway Street. Real ale buff's pub serving Stoke-on-Trent brewed "Titanic" beers. Food and accommodation. Tel: 01785 253313.

Good shopping centre featuring all the well known 'high street' names plus many attractive individual shops tucked away down twisting side streets. Indoor market Tue, Thur, Fri & Sat.

i TOURIST INFORMATION - Market Street. Tel: 01785 619619.

BUSES - Midland Red and Potteries Motor Traction. Tel: 0870 608 2 608.

TRAINS - Important railhead with wide variety of services. Tel: 08457 484950.

STOKE PRIOR Map 14

One of three scattered villages sharing their prefix, Stoke Prior is familiar to many canal holidaymakers as the headquarters of Black Prince Holidays. Their offices overlook Lock 44.

QUEENS HEAD - canalside Bridge 48. Immensely popular country pub, sleek of ambience and slick of service. Massive, but inexpensive, portions from a carvery style restaurant. Payphone and garden. Families welcome. Tel: 01527 877777.

THE NAVIGATION - adjacent Bridge 44. Open all day, food.Tel: 01527 870194.

i AVONCROFT - 1 mile west of Bridge 48. Fascinating museum of buildings which have escaped demolition and been given sanctuary on quiet Worcestershire hillside. Open daily throughout the summer and on selected winter days. Tel: 01527 831886 for further details.

STOKE WORKS Map 15

Prosaically named after the enormous salt works, now demolished and replaced by a high-tech latex plant, this one of the Stokes is a useful mooring point.

BOAT & RAILWAY - canalside Bridge 42. Highly regarded pub amongst the canal fraternity. Banks's beers, bar meals Mon-Sat. Nice waterside terrace. Tel: 01527 831065.

General store, post office and butcher half a mile west of Bridge 42, say 10 minutes walk.

TAXIS - local taxi operator, Clearway of Catshill, took the trouble to contact us, pointing out that they regularly ferry boaters from the canal at Stoke Works into Bromsgrove for shopping or to the Avoncroft Museum. Tel: 01527 872556.

STOURBRIDGE Map 33

From the canal wharf, it's but a short walk through the underpass beneath the ring-road (which encircles the glass-making town of Stourbridge like a boa constrictor) to the town centre. And how unexpected! For Stourbridge is not yet another Black Country industrial community, but rather a market town with a profusion of shops and some not uninteresting architecture. Even the usually restrained Pevsner was moved to label the former grammar school (on your left as you ascend the High Street) 'picturesque', whilst a little further on stands the town clock; imposing, fluted-columned, cast in the local iron works in 1857, and equipped with a match-striking plate (a typical piece of Victorian thoughtfulness and ingenuity) for passers by.

MOORINGS TAVERN - Cosy local on main road to rear of town wharf. Chinese takeaway next door. Tel: 01384 374124.

FRENCH CONNECTION - Coventry Street (opposite the town clock). Appealing bistro. Tel: 01384 390940.

ROYAL EXCHANGE - Enville Street. Batham's tied house offering only snacks to deflect from the serious business of downing this wonderful Black Country brew. Tel: 01384 396726.

SAMSON & LION - canalside Lock 4 of Stourbridge flight. Banks's and Marstons beers, good food and a friendly atmosphere. Skittle alley and garden with aviary. Tel: 01384 77796.

Stourbridge has a daily market, whilst two precincts play host to all the major chain stores. Make your way to the FRENCH CONNECTION

continued on page 88

continued from page 87

delicatessen on Coventry Street where you'll find a mouthwatering selection of meats and regional cheeses on sale. Also noteworthy is NICKOLLS & PERKS wine merchants established as long ago as 1797.

(i) STUART CRYSTAL - Red House Glassworks, adjacent Lock 12 of Stourbridge flight. Factory tours, museum and shop. Special moorings for boating visitors. Tel: 01384 828282.

BROADFIELD HOUSE GLASS MUSEUM - Kingswinford, accessible by bus from Stourbridge. Tel: 01384 273011.

FELLOWS, MORTON & CLAYTON - boat trips along the Stourbridge Canal from the town wharf. Tel: 01384 375912.

STOURBRIDGE NAVIGATION TRUST - Tel: 01384 395216. Administrators of town wharf and bonded warehouse. Contact for long term mooring details, hire of hall etc.

BUSES - services throughout the area from bus station at top of High Street.

TRAINS - shuttle service on Britain's shortest branch line between Stourbridge Town and Stourbridge Junction for connections to Birmingham and Worcester. Tel: 0121-200 2700 for bus and train timetable information.

STOURPORT Map 1

Water on the brain has left Stourport under the illusion that it's a coastal resort. All the trappings are here: funfairs and fish & chips, steamer trips, paddling pools and amusement arcades. Day trippers pour in from the West Midlands to let their hair down and make believe they are really in Rhyl. Marginally more in touch with reality, us boaters can swagger about the town pretending that we've just come up with a cargo of oil from Avonmouth.

THE ANGEL - riverside. Tel: 01299 822661. Lively local on the riverbank.

RISING SUN - canalside Bridge 5A. Tel: 01299 822530. Quaint little Banks's backstreet local offering good value meals.

SWAN HOTEL - High Street. Tel: 01299 822483. Bar and restaurant meals.

BIRD IN HAND - canalside between bridges 7 and 8. Tel: 01299 822385. Bar meals, outdoor seating beside the canal on summer days, bowling green.

OLD CROWN - Bridge Street. Tel: 01299 825693. Wetherspoon pub with patio overlooking basins. Wide choice of food and real ales.

LOCK SHOP TEAROOM - canalside York Street Lock. Tel: 01299 829442. *Numerous other eating and drinking establishments as befits this inland resort. More fish & chip bars than you would imagine sustainable.*

The town centre is large enough to support branches of Boots, Woolworths and W.H.Smith. The 'big four' banks have branches, all with auto-tellers. There are KwikSave and Lidl supermarkets within easy reach of the canal, but much more homely is the LOCK SHOP by York Street Lock, open daily until late, and pleasantly disposed towards boaters' obscure needs.

BUSES - frequent "Wyre Shuttle" services to Kidderminster. Tel: 01345 212555.

SWINDON Map 4

Not easily confused with its Wiltshire namesake - once you've seen it anyway - this Swindon barely amounts to more than a spattering of houses at a meeting of by-roads and a small housing estate occupying the site of a former steel works. To the west lies Highgate Common, threaded by the "Staffordshire Way", and, not far beyond - should you have the benefit of bicycles - Halfpenny Green and its vineyard.

NAVIGATION INN - adjacent Greens-forge Lock. One of the most comfortable of inns on the southern half of the Staffs & Worcs Canal. Food, Banks's & Bass. Families welcome. Most boaters opt for this in preference to Swindon's four other pubs, though we have always had a soft spot for the tiny GREEN MAN just west of Bridge 40. Fish & chips & doner kebab in Swindon itself.

The only chance to shop between Kinver and the outskirts of Wolverhampton, Swindon offers a post office store with off licence and a general store and newsagent. And boy, doesn't it feel good to be beyond the siren call of a supermarket for at least a day!

TARDEBIGGE *Map 14*

The 18th century church with its slender 135ft spire is a local landmark and is worth climbing the hillside to view at closer quarters. The canal yard is equally pleasing, its employees cottages exuding considerable charm. There are no shops, but buses will whisk you into Bromsgrove. Canalside, the former pumping engine house has been converted into TYLERS LOCK pub/restaurant.

TIBBERTON *Map 16*

Nondescript village, but the provision of good visitor moorings adds to the attraction of its two pleasant Banks's pubs, both of which do food, whilst the small post office stores provides useful emergency rations, newspapers etc on a daily basis, though mornings only Wed, Sat & Sun.

TIPTON *Map 8*

'Teapton' - once islanded by canals - was nicknamed the 'Venice of the Midlands' long before the hackneyed analogy of Birmingham having more canals than Venice became common currency. And even with the relegation of the Tipton Green & Toll End Communication Canal to a landscaped pathway, Owen Street (the main thoroughfare) remains embraced by the old and new main lines. The little town's most famous son is William Perry aka 'The Tipton Slasher', England's champion prizefighter for seven undefeated years from 1850. His pugilistic years followed a period as a canal boatman; ideal preparation one imagines. His statue overlooks the canal by Owen Street Bridge.

THE FOUNTAIN - Owen Street. Once the Slasher's headquarters, now a Banks's pub offering food and a canalside beer garden.
PAPA PICCOLO'S PIZZERIA - dial a pizza on 0121 557 8555.
Two fish & chip shops and a Chinese takeaway.

A handy little shopping centre easily reached from either of the main lines. There is an HSBC bank and a fair range of shops, including a Co-op and a branch of Firkins for those in dire need of a cream cake or two.

(i) BLACK COUNTRY LIVING MUSEUM - Tipton Road, Dudley. Tel: 0121-557 9643. Open daily between March and October; Wed-Sun in winter. Admission charge. Each year the disparity grows between the real West Midlands and this little pocket of preserved in aspic, nostalgia-tinted Black Country. Located on a 26 acre site, it'll take you at least a couple of hours to walk around the exhibits which include a village, colliery, pumping engine, boat dock and fairground. Trams (and sometimes trolleybuses) offer rides from the main entrance to the village. An additional attraction is the operation of electric trip boats into Dudley Tunnel and its caverns. Thoroughly recommended! Secure overnight moorings are available for visiting boaters, access via Tipton Junction.

BUSES - links from centre of Tipton to/from Dudley (an interesting town with a castle to visit) also calling at stops by the Black Country Museum, otherwise about 20 minutes walk from the railway station.
TRAINS - local services half-hourly between Wolverhampton and Birmingham.
Tel: 0121-200 2700 for details of local bus and train services.

WALSALL *Map 36*

You cannot go far in Walsall without discovering the town's stock in trade, leather goods; especially saddle making. Walsall is also a centre for lorinery (saddle ironmongery) and is esteemed throughout the world for such equipment, particularly in South America, where no self-respecting Pampas gaucho would be seen dead without an elegant pair of spurs cast in this North Black Country metropolis. Walsall is inordinantly proud of two former citizens. A statue on 'The Bridge' (which recalls that Flean Brook once flowed visibly through the town) salutes Sister Dora, an Anglican nun who arrived in Walsall in 1865. She found the medical facilities primitive, many industrial accidents turning to fatalities for the want of treatment. She devoted the rest of her life to local people, rushing to the scene of industrial disasters, coping with a smallpox epidemic, and providing solace and succour to the working men and their families to such an extent that she has never been forgotten. Her statue is notable in being the first in England erected to a woman other than a monarch. The base features copper friezes depicting her work against suitably satanic industrial backdrops. Walsall's other hero is Jerome K. Jerome who was born in the town, but whose family was forced to move following his father's bankruptcy when JKJ was only two. Jerome didn't return to Walsall until he was sixty, coming first to collect material for his autobiography, and then to receive the Freedom of the Borough. A man capable of the delicious humour of *Three Men in a Boat* must have enjoyed the gentle irony of that moment; many larger towns have done less to honour greater men. When the nights draw in, West Midlanders leave summer behind with a barely perceptible sigh and turn their thoughts to the 'Walsall Illuminations'. Quarter of a million Black Country folk pour into the Arboretum, where 40,000 light bulbs temporarily transform 35 acres of parkland into a carnival atmosphere rivalling Blackpool's.

continued on page 90

continued from page 89

THE WHARF 10 - canalside Town Wharf. Lively cafe/bar beside the refurbished basin and overlooked by the new, much vaunted art gallery. Sandwiches, salads and pastas. Local Highgate Brewery beers on draught.
THE GEORGE STEPHENSON - canalside, Birchills. Risibly misnamed (on account, one assumes, of the neighbouring trackbed of the Midland Railway's long defunct Walsall-Wolverhampton line) modern all-day pub catering for all the family.

Walsall's thriving market is held on Tuesdays, Fridays and Saturdays and attracts shoppers from all over the region. There are several busy precincts burgeoning with all the usual chain stores. The Guildhall has been attractively converted as a centre for craft and gift shops, as has the nearby Mews in Goodhall Street.

(i) WALSALL LEATHER CENTRE - Wisemore, Walsall. Open Tue-Sat 10-5, Sun 12-5, plus Bank Hol Mons. Displays of Walsall's leather-making history, demonstrations of saddle-making etc. Tel: 01922 721153.
THE NEW ART GALLERY - Gallery Square. Open Tue-Sun admission free. Tel: 01922 654400. Spanking new gallery with a surprisingly cosmopolitan range of exhibits by the likes of Cezanne, Van Gogh, Renoir and Picasso.
JEROME K. JEROME BIRTHPLACE MUSEUM - Bradford Street. Open Tue-Sat admission free. Tel: 01922 728860.

BUSES - Services throughout the region from striking new bus station. Useful towpath-walking links with Brownhills etc.
TRAINS - local services to/from Stafford, Wolverhampton and Birmingham. Details of buses and trains on 0121-200 2700.

WEDNESFIELD Map 35

The big brick church of St Thomas, topped by a gold cockerel weathervane, lures you off the cut into Wednesfield's busy main street. Strange how these tangential Black Country communities contrive to stay so busy. This town's particular contribution to the industrial revolution was in the painful art of trap-making. Facilities are more ambitious than you'd think: banks, a retail market on Tue, Fri & Sat and a Sainsburys by Rookery Bridge. BENTLEY BRIDGE retail park offers eating places and a cinema complex.

WHITTINGTON Map 24

Attractive village retaining three pubs, a Chinese take-away, a Co-op store, pharmacy and newsagent. Buses to Lichfield.

WOLVERHAMPTON Map 7

Disembarking at the commendable moorings above the top lock, boaters visiting Wolverhampton might well be pleasantly surprised by the size and scope of the town which, in common with other proud Black Country boroughs, has a tendency to languish in shadows cast by Big Brother Birmingham. Wulfrunians will rapidly put you right. After all, their pedigree is more impressive than that of the upstart down the A41. Ethelred the Unready granted the town a charter in 985 - Birmingham had to wait two more centuries before being so recognised. In medieval times Wolverhampton was something of a wool centre, a way of life recalled by street names like Farmers Fold and Woolpack Alley, but the discovery of coal and iron turned Wolverhampton into a manufacturing town famous for lock making (notably Chubbs, whose huge triangular works overlooks the canal, though it is now in use as an arts centre), metal toys, hardware and belt buckles. Today, like everywhere else, Wolverhampton has had to re-gear for the future, though steel is still processed in the periphery of heavy industry which still cloaks the town. One of the saddest industrial victims of recent years is the disused Springfield Brewery, visibly deteriorating from the Twenty-One.

GREAT WESTERN - Sun Street. Tel : 01902 351090. Adjacent old Low Level station. Easiest access from canal by Broad Street Bridge. Go under railway then turn right past old station until the pub comes into sight. Railway memorabilia, Bathams, Holdens, Black Country cooking (at lunchtimes), what more could you want from a pub!

continued on page 91

continued from page 90

🚂 The Mander and Wulfrun centres are modern precincts emblazoning all the inevitable names in plastic facia. But down sidestreets and up alleyways plenty of characterful local shops are waiting to be discovered by the discerning shopper. Try the faggots at any butcher, they are a Black Country delicacy - really! Devastatingly, the most distinctive shop of all, SNAPES tea & coffee merchants on Queen Street, has closed down.

ⓘ TOURIST INFORMATION CENTRE - 18 Queen Square. Tel: 01902 312051.

🚌 BUSES & TRAINS - respective stations directly adjacent to the canal, access via Broad Street Bridge. Local services on 0121 200 2700. Treat yourself to a ride on the new Metro tramway, a fascinating journey across what's left of the industrial Black Country! Other trains 08457 484950.

WOLSELEY *Map 27*

Roadside community on a roundabout at the junction of the A513 and A51 main roads, but more idyllic - especially when viewed from the canal - than that description suggests. Moor by Bridge 70 and you can visit a garden centre, gallery, antiques showroom and craft units, whilst the WOLSELEY ARMS (a meeting place for the T&M's promoters) is a pleasant country pub offering a wide choice of food. Tel: 01889 575133. The neighbouring SHIMLA PALACE Indian restaurant and takeaway caters for spicier tastes. Tel: 01889 881325.

WORCESTER *Map 17*

Descending from Birmingham to Worcester, the West Midlands are left intuitively behind, and you find yourself in streets where the patois has a distinct West Country burr. Royal Worcester suffered more than most at the hands of the developers during the Sixties (Ian Nairn, the late architectural writer and broadcaster, was incensed) but much making of amends has been done in recent years to enhance the city's fabric. The Cathedral, gazing devoutly over the Severn, belongs - along with Gloucester and Hereford - to a golden triangle of ecclesiastical paragons which share Europe's oldest music festival, 'The Three Choirs'. From the deep well of Worcester's history you can draw inspiration from almost any era that captures your imagination. This was the 'faithful city' of the Civil War from which Charles II escaped following the final defeat of the Cavaliers. It was the home, for much of his life, of Sir Edward Elgar. Home too of the manufacturers of Royal Worcester porcelain and that ensign of the empire, Lea & Perrins sauce. And here you'll find one of the country's loveliest cricketing venues, Worcestershire's New Road ground. So in any boating itinerary, Worcester deserves to be allotted at least half a day in your schedule.

🫖 BROWNS RESTAURANT - Quay Street. Tel: 01905 26263. Worth blowing the budget here (lunch Tue-Fri & Sun approx £20, dinner Tue-Sat approx £35) for the ambience (former riverside mill) let alone quality of the cooking.

LITTLE SAUCE FACTORY - London Road, 5 minutes walk south from Sidbury Lock. Tel: 01905 350159. Former Little Pub Co. establishment remodelled by an award-winning chef into a restaurant bar, but happily retaining the Worcester Sauce memorabilia.

CROMWELLS PANTRY - The Commandery. Coffees, teas, light snacks in adjunct to museum. Canalside or courtyard al fresco on warm days.

MCTAFFISH - Spick & span fish & chip parlour + Spice Wok by Sidbury Lock - Tel: 01905 359329.

THE ANCHOR - Diglis Basin. Down to earth Banks's boozer for prodigious swallowers and Amazons only.

🚂 Worcester is an excellent city in which to shop. Two refurbished shopping areas are The Hopmarket and Crown Passage. The Shambles, Friar Street and New Street feature numerous fascinating little shops and small businesses. Crown Gate is the main shopping precinct with adjoining street markets on Tue, Wed, Fri & Sat. If you are making the faux pas of boating through non-stop, then a number of useful provisions shops can be reached from Sidbury Lock.

ⓘ TOURIST INFORMATION CENTRE - The Guildhall, High Street. Tel: 01905 726311. Worcester appears to have more visitor centres than any other provincial city of its size. A thorough list defies our space limitations, but obvious highlights are: THE COMMANDERY (canalside by Sidbury Lock) which was Charles II's headquarters during the Civil War; ROYAL WORCESTER (Severn Street, near Sidbury Lock again), the porcelain and bone china makers; and THE CATHEDRAL, dating from the 11th century and the burial place of King John. Incidentally, if you are moored in the vicinity of Sidbury, we can thoroughly recommend a stroll in Fort Royal Park, the top of which offers splendid views across the city towards the Malvern Hills.

🚌 BUSES - Midland Red West services throughout the area and local Citibus services. Tel: 01905 763888.

TRAINS - stations at Foregate Street and Shrub Hill. Services to/from the Malverns (nice idea for an excursion), Droitwich, Kidderminster, Birmingham etc. Tel: 08457 484950.

How to use the Maps

There are forty-one numbered maps whose layout is shown by the Route Planner inside the front cover. Maps 1-19 show the route of the STOURPORT RING; and Maps 7-10 and 20-32 the route of the BLACK COUNTRY RING. Maps 33/34 cover the Stourbridge and Dudley Canals, whilst Maps 35-41 cover the northern area of the Birmingham Canal Navigations.

The maps are easily read in either direction. The simplest way of progressing from map to map is to proceed to the next map numbered (in orange figures) from the edge of the map you are on. Figures quoted at the top of each map refer to distance per map, locks per map and average cruising times. An alternative indication of timings from centre to centre can be found on the Route Planner. Obviously, cruising times vary with the nature of your boat and the number of crew at your disposal, so quoted times should be taken only as an estimate. Neither do times quoted take into account any delays which might occur at lock flights in high season.

Using the Text

Each map is accompanied by a route commentary. Details of most settlements passed through are given alphabetically in the Gazetteer. Regular readers will already be familiar with our somewhat irreverent approach. But we 'tell it as we find it', in the belief that the users of this guide will find this attitude more valuable than a strict towing of the tourist publicity line.

Towpath Walking

The simplest way to go canal exploring is on foot. It costs largely nothing and you are free to concentrate on the passing scene; something that boaters are not always at liberty to do. With the exception of the River Severn, all the waterways covered by this guide are equipped with towpaths. Over the years we have walked every yard of these, and we try to keep our towpath information as up to date as possible. We recommend the use of public transport to facilitate 'one-way' walking and suggest that this is used on the outward leg of an itinerary so that you are not necessarily pressured to complete the walk within a certain time limit. We also stress the advisability of using our quoted telephone numbers to check up to the minute details of bus and train services.

Towpath Cycling

Cycling canal towpaths is an increasingly popular activity, but one that British Waterways - the nationalised body responsible for the upkeep of the bulk of Britain's navigable inland waterways - is only slowly coming to terms with. The goalposts keep moving, but as we went to press it was still necessary for cyclists wishing to use towpaths to acquire a permit (albeit a free of charge one) from one of the British Waterways offices listed opposite.

Boating

Boating on inland waterways is an established, though relatively small, facet of the UK holiday industry. There are over 20,000 privately owned boats registered on the canals, but in addition to these numerous firms offer boats for hire. These companies range from small operators with half a dozen boats to sizeable fleets run by companies with several bases.

Most hire craft have all the creature comforts you are likely to expect. In the excitement of planning a boating holiday you may give scant thought to the contents of your hire boat, but at the end of a hard day's boating such matters take on more significance, and a well equipped, comfortable boat, large enough to accommodate your crew, can make the difference between a good holiday and an indifferent one.

Traditionally, hire boats are booked out by the week or fortnight, though many firms now offer more flexible short breaks or extended weeks. All reputable hire firms give newcomers tuition in boat handling and lock working, and first-timers soon find themselves adapting to the pace of things 'on the cut'.

Navigational Advice

LOCKS are part of the charm of canal cruising, but they are potentially dangerous environments for children, pets and careless adults. Use of them should be methodical and unhurried, whilst special care should be exercised in rain, frost and snow when slippery hazards abound. We have no space here for detailed instructions on lock operation: trusting that if you own your boat you will, by definition, already be experienced in canal cruising; whilst first time hire boaters should be given tuition in the operation of locks before they set out.

Apart from the basin locks at Diglis, Worcester and the automated locks on the River Severn between Worcester and Stourport, all the locks on the canals covered by this guide are of the familiar narrow-beam variety. All gates should be closed on leaving each chamber (unless courteously leaving them open for an approaching boat) and all paddles wound down.

The River Severn locks at Bevere, Holt and Lincomb are mechanised and manned. One prolonged blast on the boat horn should be enough to alert the keeper that you wish to use the lock, though in most cases he will already be aware via the lock-keeper's grapevine of your approach. Be guided by the colour light signals, but wait for the signal to turn green and the gates to open before approaching too closely. The chambers of these locks are large and you may be sharing with other craft. Steadying straps and chains are attached to the chamber walls and these can be hand held to control your boat if there is any turbulence. Always follow the lock-keeper's advice. He will be in his control cabin as you pass through the lock.

The basin locks at Worcester and Stourport are only open during timetabled hours - as indeed are the river locks mentioned above. Hire craft are likely to have up to date timings in their boat manuals, but private boaters can obtain details from British Waterways, Llanthony Warehouse, Gloucester GL1 2EJ. Tel: 01452 318000.

MOORING on the canals featured in this guide is per usual practice - ie on the towpath side, away from sharp bends, bridge-holes and narrows. An 'open' bollard symbol represents visitor mooring sites; either as designated specifically by British Waterways or, in some cases, as recommended by our own personal experience. Of course, one of the great joys of canal boating has always been the ability to moor wherever (sensibly) you like. In recent years, however, it has become obvious, particularly in urban areas, that there are an increasing number of undesirable locations where mooring is not to be recommended for fear of vandalism, theft or abuse. We hope, therefore, that you find our suggestions both pleasant and secure. But do bear in mind that the absence of a bollard symbol from any particular location does not necessarily imply that it is unsuitable or not to be recommended.

FLOODS can occur on the River Severn at any time of year at short notice. Officials should be on hand to help and advise at such times. If you are already on the river you must tie up at the nearest official moorings and remain there until further notice. At times of flood you may be denied access to the river. Boat hire companies are familiar with the Severn's moods and will be sympathetic to genuine delays. If you have any enquiries regarding flood levels contact the Environment Agency's 'Floodline' on 0845 9881188 or speak to a duty officer on 0121-711 2324.

CLOSURES (or 'stoppages' in canal parlance) traditionally occur on the inland waterways between November and April, during which time most of the heavy maintenance work is undertaken. Occasionally, however, an emergency stoppage, or perhaps a water restriction, may be imposed at short notice, closing part of the route you intend to use. Up to date details are usually available from hire bases. Alternatively, British Waterways provide a recorded message service for private boaters. The number to ring is: 01923 201401/2. Stoppages are also listed on British Waterways' internet site: www.britishwaterways.co.uk

Emergencies

British Waterways operate a central emergency telephone service. Dial the operator and ask for FREEPHONE CANALS. For mobile users the number is 01384 215785.

Useful Contacts

British Waterways Midlands & South West Region Peel's Wharf, Fazeley, Tamworth, Staffs B78 3QZ. Tel: 01827 252000. Fax: 01827 288071.
British Waterways Birmingham & Black Country Ocker Hill, Tipton. Tel: 0121-506 1300. Fax: 0121-506 1313.

Societies

The Inland Waterways Association was founded in 1946 to campaign for retention of the canal system. Many routes now open to pleasure boaters may not have been so but for this organisation. Membership details may be obtained from: Inland Waterways Association, PO Box 114, Rickmansworth WD3 1ZY. Tel: 01923 711114. The current Membership Secretary of the Birmingham Canal Navigations Society can be emailed at martin@bcn-society.fsnet.co.uk The Dudley Canal Trust is based at the Blowers Green Pumphouse, Peartree Lane, Dudley, West Midlands DY2 0XP Tel: 01384 236275.

Acknowledgements

All the usual suspects! Brian Collings for the umpteenth cover; Jackie and Karen for updates; Toby Bryant; Giampiero Logiduce and all at STIGE.

Boating Facilities

Hire Bases with boating facilities

ALVECHURCH BOAT CENTRES - Worcester & Birmingham Canal Map 13. Scarfield Wharf, Alvechurch, Worcestershire B48 7SQ. Tel: 0121-445 2909. Fax: 0121-447 7120. www.alvechurch.com

ANGLO WELSH WATERWAY HOLIDAYS - Worcs & Birmingham Canal Map 17 and Staffs & Worcs Canal Map 28. 5 Portland Place, Pritchard Street, Bristol BS2 8RH. Tel: 0117 9240332. Fax: 0117 9240202.

ASSOCIATED CRUISERS - BCN Map 7. Little's Lane, Wolverhampton WV1 1JJ. Tel: 01902 23673.

BLACK PRINCE HOLIDAYS - Worcester & Birmingham Canal Map 14. Stoke Prior, Bromsgrove, Worcestershire B60 4LA. Tel: 01527 575115. Fax: 01527 575116.

BROOK LINE - Worcester & Birmingham Canal Map 16. Dunhampstead Wharf, Oddingley, Droitwich, Worcs. WR9 7JX Tel: 01905 773889.

SHERBORNE WHARF - BCN Maps 11 & 20. Sherborne Street, Birmingham B16 8DE. Tel: 0121-455 6163. Fax: 0121-455 6262. www.sherbornewharf.co.uk

STROUDWATER CRUISERS - Staffs & Worcs Canal Map 1. Engine Lane, Stourport, Worcs DY13 9EP. Tel: 01299 877222. Fax: 01299 824021.

SWAN LINE CRUISERS - Trent & Mersey Canal Map 25. Fradley Junction, Alrewas, Burton-on-Trent DE13 7DN. Tel: 01283 790332.

TEDDESLEY BOAT COMPANY - Staffs & Worcs Canal Map 30. Teddesley Road, Penkridge, Stafford ST19 5RH. Tel: 01785 714692. Fax: 01785 714894. www.narrowboats.co.uk

VIKING AFLOAT - Worcs & Birmingham Canal Map 17 and Staffs & Worcs Canal Map 31. Lowesmoor Wharf, Worcester WR1 2RS. Tel: 01905 610660. Fax: 01905 616715. www.viking-afloat.com

WATER TRAVEL - Staffs & Worcs Canal Map 7. Oxley Moor Road, Wolverhampton WV9 5HW. Tel: 01902 782371.

Hire Agency

HOSEASONS HOLIDAYS Sunway House, Lowestoft, Suffolk NR32 2LW. Tel: 01502 501010. Fax: 01502 586781. www.hoseasons.co.uk

Boatyards with no weekly hire facilities

ALDRIDGE MARINA - Wyrley & Essington Map 38.Tel: 01922 453397

ANGLESEY BRIDGE MARINA - Wyrley & Essington Canal Map 37. Tel: 01543 454994.

CALF HEATH MARINA - Staffs & Worcs Canal Map 31. Tel: 01902 790570.

CANAL TRANSPORT SERVICES - Cannock Extension Canal Map 37. Tel: 01543 374370.

DEBBIES DAY BOATS - Birmingham & Fazeley Canal Map 23. Tel: 01827 262042.

HANBURY WHARF CANAL VILLAGE - Worcs & Birmingham Canal Map 15. Tel: 01905 771018.

FAZELEY MILL MARINA - Birmingham & Fazeley Canal Map 23. Tel: 01827 261138.

JD BOAT SERVICES - Staffs & Worcs Canal Map 31. Tel: 01902 791811. Fax: 01902 791446.

KINGS BROMLEY WHARF - Trent & Mersey Canal Map 25. Tel: 01543 417209.

LIMEKILN NARROWBOATS - Staffs & Worcs Canal Map 6. Tel/Fax: 01902 751147.

OLDBURY BOAT SERVICES - BCN Map 9. Tel: 0121 544 1795.

OXLEY MARINE - Staffs & Worcs Canal Map 7. Tel: 01902 789522.

OTHERTON BOAT HAVEN - Staffs & Worcs Canal Map 30. Tel: 01785 712515. Fax: 01785 713849.

SEVERN VALLEY BOAT CENTRE - Staffs & Worcs Canal Map 1. Tel: 01299 871165. Fax: 01299 827211. www.severnboat.co.uk

STREETHAY WHARF - Coventry Canal Map 25. Tel/Fax: 01543 414808.

Boating Web Sites

British Waterways: www.britishwaterways.co.uk

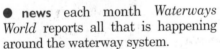